"Many books have been written to tell you how to make money, save money, and invest money. Now there's a book that can tell you how to spend it. Wisely."

Chip Heath, co-author of *Decisive: How to Make Better Decisions in Life and Work*

Happy Money

The New Science of Smarter Spending

Elizabeth Dunn & Michael Norton

A Oneworld Book

This edition published by Oneworld Publications in 2014

First published in Great Britain and the Commonwealth by
Oneworld Publications in 2013

Originally published in the US by Simon & Schuster 2013

A CIP record for this title is available from the British Library

ISBN 978-1-78074-337-0
ISBN 978-1-78074-223-6 (ebook)

Designed by Akasha Archer
Printed and bound in Denmark by Nørhaven A/S

Oneworld Publications
10 Bloomsbury Street
London, WC1B 3SR
England

To my mother, Winifred Brand,
who taught me my first lessons in happiness.
—Liz

To my grandmother, Delia Irwin,
who taught me that there's more to being happy than being smart.
—Mike

Contents

Prologue xi

1. Buy Experiences 1

2. Make It a Treat 27

3. Buy Time 53

4. Pay Now, Consume Later 79

5. Invest in Others 105

Epilogue: Zooming Out 135

Notes 159

Acknowledgments 183

Index 187

Happy Money

Prologue

After a decade spent earning degrees, Elizabeth Dunn experienced a major life change. She started earning money. As a young professor, Liz suddenly skyrocketed all the way to an average adult income, and began to wonder what to do with her newfound wealth. Having just completed her Ph.D. in social psychology, Liz did what only a true academic would: she turned to the scientific literature for guidance. She found about seventeen thousand articles on the relationship between money and happiness, many of which seemed to suggest that additional income provides surprisingly little additional happiness.* But, she wondered, just because money often fails to buy happiness, does that mean that it *can't*? What if people spent their money differently—and better?

Liz called up her friend Michael Norton. The two had met during their postgraduate years, at an academic summer camp (think band camp—but nerdier). Liz admired Mike's willingness to tackle wacky questions, such as "How do people think wealth should be distributed?" and "At what age do kids become hypocrites?" In his postcamp years—and to the surprise

* Any sentence summarizing so many papers likely contains an oversimplification. For a more in-depth discussion of this complex and contentious literature, we suggest *Happiness: Unlocking the Mysteries of Psychological Wealth*, by Ed Diener and Robert Biswas-Diener.

of his entire extended family—Mike had become a professor at Harvard Business School.

Both gainfully employed for the first time, we decided to work together to understand what grown-ups usually do with their money. Most importantly, we wanted to know if people could spend their money in less typical, but happier ways. Together we started doling out cash to strangers. But there was a catch: rather than letting them spend it however they wanted, we made them spend it how *we* wanted. We'll tell you the whole story later in the book, but our first discoveries were promising: changing the way people spent their money altered their happiness over the course of the day. And we saw this effect even when people spent as little as $5. Since then we have expanded and broadened our research on the science of spending to diverse regions of the world, from Belgium to East Africa. We have taken our work "under the skin," demonstrating that everyday spending choices unleash a cascade of biological and emotional effects—detectable right down to saliva. And we have worked with organizations ranging from a recreational dodge ball league to the number-one restaurant in the world—Ferran Adrià's elBulli—to examine how shifting the way individuals spend money influences the success of teams and companies.

Our research has been featured in media outlets ranging from the *Guardian* and *Harvard Business Review* to the *Hindustan Times* and *The Tonight Show with Jay Leno.* One fun side benefit of this media exposure is that we often get feedback from self-appointed pundits. The comments below appeared in response to a CNN.com story covering some of our research:[1]

> If I won the lottery I would take it upon myself to try and teach people the value of money. For example, I would walk up to people on the street and hold out a couple hundred bucks and say "Here, you want this!" When they reached for it I would yank it back and be like . . . "Yeah right! What are you crazy? Do you think that people just wake up and get handed huge sums of money!" Of course I wouldn't tell them that I won the lottery because that kind of defeats the lesson I'm trying to convey.

> I would just build a fort, completely made of money, and hide in it.

> I would fill a big bath tub with money and get in the tub while smoking a big fat cigar and sipping a glass of champagne. Then I'd have a picture taken and dozens of 8x10 glossies made. Anyone begging for money or trying to extort from me would receive a copy of the picture and nothing else.

> When I win I am going to buy my own little mountain and have a little house on top.

These diverse plans share two striking similarities: these would-be lottery winners planned to use the money for *stuff* (forts, champagne, and mountains) for themselves and themselves *alone* (taunting others and buying isolation). As it turns out, some of these schemes are not just unproductive for happiness, but *counterproductive*. Shifting from buying stuff to buying experiences, and from spending on yourself to spending on others, can have a dramatic impact on happiness.

Why Focus on Spending Differently Rather than Earning More?

Every large bookshop has a shelf filled with books designed to help you get more money. By focusing on how to spend the money you have rather than how to accumulate more of it, our perspective departs from the obsession with chasing increased wealth in the pursuit of happiness. New research shows that greater wealth often fails to provide as much happiness as many people expect. In a national sample of Americans, individuals thought that their satisfaction with life would double if they made $55,000 rather than $25,000: twice as much money, twice as much happy.[2] But the data revealed that people who earned $55,000 were only 9 percent more satisfied than those making $25,000. Around the world, income has surprisingly little influence on whether people smile, laugh, and experience enjoyment on a typical day.[3] And in the United States, once people are earning around $75,000 per year, making more money has *no impact at all* on their day-to-day feelings of happiness.[4]

Although money can provide all kinds of wonderful things, from tastier food to safer neighborhoods, wealth comes at a cost. Just thinking about wealth can push us away from the kinds of behaviors that promote happiness—such as playing nicely with others.[5] In one study, students received a big stack of Monopoly money and spent several minutes imagining a wealthy future.[6] Other students were left with no Monopoly money and spent time thinking about their plans for the next day. Suddenly a research assistant stumbled in front of them, spilling pencils everywhere. Students with the stack of cash picked up fewer pencils. In another study, individuals who merely saw a photograph of money preferred solitary activities, choosing personal cooking classes over a catered dinner with friends. This research helps to explain why our would-be lottery winners sought isolation. Just being reminded of wealth can propel people to distance themselves from others, undermining happiness.

Even though we've read all of the relevant research, and conducted some of it ourselves, we haven't turned down any raises. So, rather than suggest that you stop trying to get more money, our goal is to help you use the money you have to get more happiness. And insights into how to make yourself happier are also relevant for any organization in the business of trying to make *others* happy. We'll offer guidance on structuring employee and customer experiences to create the largest impact on their happiness and satisfaction. Whether you're a massage therapist, travel agent, or CEO, we'll help you provide your colleagues and clients with the most happiness for every pound you spend on them—and for every pound they spend with you.

The Principles

In each chapter, we'll focus on one of five key principles of happy money and help you understand how, when, and why it works so that you can apply it in your personal and professional life.

- *Buy Experiences (Chapter One).* The vast majority of Britons aspire to own their own home.[7] But recent research suggests that home ownership and happiness don't necessarily correlate. Material things (from beautiful homes to fancy pens) turn out to provide less happiness than experiential purchases (like trips, concerts, and special meals). Whether you're spending £2 or £200,000, buying experiences rather than material goods can inoculate you against buyer's remorse. Not all experiences are created equal, and we'll highlight the kinds of experiences, large and small, most likely to provide happiness. Surprisingly, even experiences that seem a little painful can produce lasting pleasure. We'll show how, by harnessing the power of experiences, an entrepreneur named Will Dean convinced people to pay him for the privilege of crawling through pits of mud.

- *Make It a Treat (Chapter Two).* Many residents of London have never visited Big Ben. What stops them? When something wonderful is always available, people are less inclined to appreciate it. Limiting our access to the things we like best may help to "re-virginize" us, renewing our capacity for pleasure. Rather than advocating wholesale self-denial (say, giving up coffee completely), we'll demonstrate the value of turning our favorite things back into *treats* (making that afternoon latte a special indulgence rather than a daily necessity). We'll show how to apply this principle to purchases major and mundane, and we'll profile creative companies that have transformed products ranging from rental cars to toilet paper into treats. Along the way, we'll describe new research showing that driving a luxury car provides no more happiness than an economy model, and that commercials can enhance the pleasure of television.

- *Buy Time (Chapter Three).* By permitting us to outsource our most dreaded tasks, from scrubbing toilets to cleaning gutters, money can transform the way we spend our time, freeing us to pursue our passions. Yet wealthier individuals do not spend their time in happier ways on a daily basis; thus they fail to use their money to buy themselves happier time. We'll show the wisdom of asking yourself a quick question before buying: How will this purchase change the way I use my time? When people focus on their time rather than their money, they act like scientists of happiness, choosing activities that promote their well-being. For companies, this principle entails thinking about compensation in a broader way, rewarding employees not only with money, but with time. We'll discuss how companies ranging from Intel to Patagonia to Home Depot have developed creative strategies to give even their busiest employees a sense of time affluence, a potent predictor of people's satisfaction with their jobs, and their lives.

- *Pay Now, Consume Later (Chapter Four).* In the age of the iPad, products are available instantly and our wallets are lined with plastic instead of paper. Digital technology and credit cards have encouraged us to adopt a "consume now and pay later" shopping mind-set. By putting this powerful principle into *reverse*—by paying up front and delaying consumption—you can buy more happiness, even as you spend less money. Because delaying consumption allows spenders to reap the pleasures of anticipation without the buzzkill of reality, holidays provide the most happiness *before* they occur. And research shows that waiting, even briefly, for something as simple as a piece of chocolate makes it taste better when we get it. Delays can also be a source of frustration, of course, and we'll show how businesses can stagecraft their metaphorical waiting rooms to turn customers' impatience into increased satisfaction. The benefits of delaying consumption are particularly likely to emerge when we pay up front. By paying now and consuming later, purchases ranging from makeup to mojitos can be enjoyed as though they were free. Even better, people are less prone to overspend when they experience the pain of paying up front. This pain can put them on the path to decreasing their debt, which, as we'll see, provides one of the best routes toward increased happiness.

- *Invest in Others (Chapter 5).* On a March day in 2010, two bespectacled white men sat in a corner booth of a diner in Carter Lake, Iowa. Bill Gates and Warren Buffett—two of the richest people in the world—had an idea. They would ask America's billionaires to pledge the majority of their wealth to charity. Buffett decided to donate 99 percent of his wealth, saying "I couldn't be happier with that decision."[9] While dozens of books dissect Buffett's investing habits, this chapter shows how the rest of us might learn from his *investments in others.* New research demonstrates that spending money on others provides a bigger happiness boost than spending money on yourself. And this principle holds in an extraordinary range of circumstances, from a Canadian university student purchasing a scarf for her mother to a Ugandan woman buying lifesaving malaria medication for a friend. The benefits of giving emerge among children before the age of two, and are detectable even in samples of saliva. Investing in others can make individuals feel healthier and wealthier—and can even help people win at dodge ball. We'll show how businesses like PepsiCo and Google and not-for-profits like DonorsChoose.org are harnessing these benefits by encouraging donors, customers, and employees to invest in others.

Into the Operating Room

Uniting the five principles of this book is one simple premise. Before you spend that £5 as you usually would, stop to ask yourself: Is this happy money? Am I spending this money in the way that will give me the biggest happiness bang for my buck?

When it comes to increasing the amount of money they have, most people recognize that relying on their own intuition is insufficient, spawning an entire industry of financial advisors. But when it comes to *spending* that money, people are often content to rely on their hunches about what will make them happy. And yet, if human happiness is even half as complicated as the stock market, there is little reason to assume that intuition provides a sufficient guide. Fifty years of psychological research has shown that most of the "action" in human thought and emotion takes place beneath the level of conscious awareness[8]—and so trying to uncover the causes of your own happiness through introspection is like trying to perform your own heart transplant. You have some idea of what needs to be done, but a surgical expert would come in handy.

Consider us your surgical experts.

1

Buy Experiences

"After two or three fabulous days of preparing with your crew, you're suited up and you're raring to go. The climb to 50,000 feet is marked with quiet contemplation but there's an air of confidence and eager anticipation. Then the countdown to release, a brief moment of quiet before a wave of unimaginable but controlled power surges through the craft. . . . As you hurtle through the edges of the atmosphere, the large windows show the cobalt blue sky turning to mauve and indigo and finally to black."

This description greets visitors to Virgin Galactic's website. The company now makes it possible for you to pre-book a ticket for a six-minute spaceflight. But at $200,000 each, these tickets don't come cheap. Announcing a trip into orbit is likely to prompt some concerned looks from friends and family, looks that could be avoided by spending that $200,000 on a more traditional purchase—say, upgrading to a Tudor-style home on a leafy street in the suburbs. Even in the wake of the recent housing meltdown, most people would advocate the purchase of the upgraded homestead over the ticket to outer space. But research on happiness points in the opposite direction.

It may be hard to see how a trip to space could be a reasonable expenditure, so let's start with the fact that buying a big, beautiful house may not be a wise use of money. Remarkably, there is almost no evidence that buying a home—or a newer, nicer home—increases happiness. Between 1991 and 2007, researchers tracked thousands of people in Germany who moved to a new house because there was something about their old house that they didn't like.[1] Immediately after settling in to their new abodes, these movers reported being much more satisfied with their new homes than they'd been with their old ones. Humans are adaptable creatures, however, and research shows that people often get used to whatever they've got. So we might expect that this initial spike in housing satisfaction would wear off, leaving people no happier with their home than they were before moving. But that's not what happened. Satisfaction with the new home only wore off a little bit, and in the subsequent five years, movers remained significantly more satisfied with their new home than they'd been with their old one. Sounds promising, but there's just one problem: while movers' satisfaction with their *houses* increased substantially, their satisfaction with their *lives*—their overall happiness—didn't improve at all.

Of course, we don't know what else was going on in their lives. We can't flip a coin and randomly assign people to live in a big, beautiful house or a cramped, unsightly one. But colleges and universities can. At Harvard, first-year students are randomly assigned to spend their second through final years living in one of twelve different houses. The houses have dining halls, courtyards, and libraries, and much of undergraduate life revolves around them. Some of the houses are beautiful, spacious, and centrally located. Others will never grace the cover of a Harvard brochure. They were built during an architectural nadir, after all the prime real estate was gone. Even happy-go-lucky Harvard first-years are haunted by the fear of "getting quadded" (Harvardese for being assigned to one of the faraway houses located in the Radcliffe Quad). The night before the administration hands out housing assignments, students can be spotted on the stately bridges spanning the Charles River, conducting elaborate rituals or quiet prayers to appease the Quad Gods to ensure themselves a spot in one of the coveted "river houses" close to campus. But does getting quadded really condemn students to three years of misery?

Once students receive their housing assignments from the Harvard equivalent of the Hogwarts Sorting Hat, they flood to the central part of campus, where upperclassmen sporting the house colors and dressed as the house mascots shout and cheer and welcome their newest members. This boisterous scene was once mistaken for an antiwar protest by a TV news crew, which broadcast footage of the Leverett House Bunny and other house mascots in a clip depicting "student activism." But what happens when the Leverett House Bunny takes off his costume and goes back to being a nerdy maths major, and the new students settle in to their assigned houses? As an undergraduate at Harvard, Liz wanted to find out. In a longitudinal study, she found that first-year students expected to be much happier living in the beautiful, centrally located houses, but students who ended up in desirable houses weren't any happier than students who had landed in undesirable houses.[2] Just like the movers in the German study, students who had moved into the desirable houses did report higher housing satisfaction. But their enhanced housing situation failed to impact their overall happiness.

These findings pose a puzzle. Long after the housing bubble burst, almost 90 percent of Americans continued to describe home ownership as a central component of the American dream, according to a 2011 nationwide poll.[3] Yet, even in the heart of middle America, housing seems to play a surprisingly small role in the successful pursuit of happiness. In a carefully controlled study of more than six hundred women in Ohio, homeowners weren't any happier than renters, though they were about twelve pounds heavier.[4] Of course, renters can sometimes save money by buying a home, and almost every real estate website offers tools to help consumers calculate the financial benefits of this trade-off. Although these tools are terrific for determining whether buying a house will turn out to be a good financial investment, buying a house often isn't a good investment in our happiness.* If the largest material purchase most of us will ever make provides no detectable benefit for our overall happiness, then it may be time to rethink our fundamental assumptions about how we use money. And for some, that may include trading a mortgage for a space suit.

* Housing is not totally irrelevant for human well-being. There is some evidence that objective housing characteristics (for example, leaking roofs, noisy neighbors) shape health outcomes and that housing quality plays a larger role in life satisfaction within relatively poor countries, such as South Africa. For a review, see Naoki Nakazato, Ulrich Schimmack, and Shigehiro Oishi. "Effect of Changes in Living Conditions on Well-Being: A Prospective Top-Down Bottom-Up Model," *Social Indicators Research* 100, no. 1 (January 1, 2011): 115–35.

Fly Me to the Moon

As a child, Marcia Fiamengo, a thirty-year-old nuclear engineer, dreamed of being an astronaut.[5] When she and her husband, John (also a nuclear engineer), first heard about Virgin Galactic, they talked about buying two tickets—when they were old and retired, since the six-figure fee was out of their price range as young professionals. Then, in 2010, Marcia's life changed in an unexpected and devastating way. John became sick and passed away. When Marcia received the money from John's life insurance policy, she couldn't imagine doing anything with it, and put it away while she grieved. And then one day it hit her: What better way to use this money than to honor their dream and buy a ticket to space? As Marcia put it, John's death reminded her that "life is short and fragile." These amazing experiences shouldn't be put off until a better time. You may never get the chance to experience them.

Even if you're not in the market for a ticket to space, try this simple exercise: Think of purchases you've made with the goal of increasing your own happiness. Consider one purchase that was a material thing, a tangible object that you could keep, like a piece of jewelry or furniture, some clothing, or a gadget. Now think about a purchase you made that gave you a life experience—perhaps a trip, a concert, or a special meal. If you're like most people, remembering the experience brings to mind friends and family, sights and smells. Which of these purchases made you happier?

Faced with this question, some 57 percent of Americans reported that the experiential purchase made them happier than the material purchase, while only 34 percent reported the opposite.[6] This difference was more pronounced among women, young people, and those living in cities and suburbs. But the same basic pattern emerged even for men, the elderly, and country dwellers. In study after study, people are in a better mood when they reflect on their experiential purchases, which they describe as "money well spent."

You don't need to spend $200,000 to capitalize on the principle of buying experiences. Studies show that even when people spend only a few dollars, they get more lasting pleasure from buying an experience such as playing a video game or listening to a song than from buying a material thing like a key chain or a picture frame.[7] Beyond tunes and trinkets, our day-to-day spending habits provide a window into the value of buying experiences. One ongoing U.S. study has tracked how much money adults over age fifty spend on just about everything, from refrigerators and rent to alcohol and art.[8] When researchers link these spending choices to happiness, only one category of spending matters. And it's not refrigerators, or even alcohol. It's what the researchers label "leisure": trips, movies, sporting events, gym memberships, and the like. People who spend more of their money on leisure report significantly greater satisfaction with their lives. Not surprisingly, the amount of money these older adults reported spending on leisure was dwarfed by the amount they spent on housing. But housing again turned out to have zero bearing on their life satisfaction.

The Story Behind the Orange Headband

Shortly after graduating from Harvard Business School, Will Dean started Tough Mudder, a company that stages races with obstacles designed by the British Special Forces. Dean describes the events as "Ironman meets Burning Man."[9] And the ten-mile Tough Mudder race is "not your average lame-ass mud run or spirit-crushing 'endurance' road race."[10] Never complained about your lame-ass mud run being too average? Clearly, Tough Mudder isn't for everyone. Competitors can display their mudderness to others by purchasing paraphernalia like T-shirts and tattoos. And then there are the headbands. Rather than medals, runners are given orange headbands and encouraged to wear them the next day, exchanging high-fives and knowing nods with fellow Tough Mudders on the street or the tube. This fuzzy piece of anti-bling creates community among participants, and this sense of social connection helps to account for not only the success of Dean's business, but also the value of experiences more broadly.*

Research shows that experiences provide more happiness than material goods in part because experiences are more likely to make us feel connected to others.[11] Intuitively recognizing the critical role of connection, Will Dean has crafted his business to maximize the social aspects of the Tough Mudder experience. At the start line, runners stand side by side and recite the Tough Mudder Pledge, promising to help others and put teamwork and camaraderie ahead of their own finish time. This philosophy extends beyond words. Some of the obstacles are designed to be nearly impossible for one individual to surmount alone. When Tough Mudder posted a message on Facebook announcing an event at a bar in New York City,

* The importance of social connection also helps to explain why moving to a nicer house often fails to enhance happiness. Fancier houses may not make you any happier unless they have nicer people inside them. In the Harvard housing study, students' overall happiness was unrelated to the physical features of the houses, but the quality of social life in the houses did predict students' happiness (and interestingly, some of the houses with the least desirable physical characteristics were known for their social traditions, like "Tequila Tuesdays").

more than six hundred people showed up—with just one day's notice. While Dean says that most people sign up for their first Tough Mudder event to give themselves something to train for (or because "they want to play in the mud"), it's the social connection that keeps them coming back. And they come back in droves. Over half the people who complete a Tough Mudder event return for another, often bringing friends as new recruits. Despite beginning with an advertising budget of only $8,000, the company amassed more than 800,000 Facebook fans in just two years, and now hosts sold-out events all over North America, with new events scheduled in cities from London to Tokyo.

The viral nature of Tough Mudder also grows from another source: its capacity to provide participants with a good story. Explaining the disillusionment that prompted him to start Tough Mudder, Dean says, "The thing I really disliked about triathlons and marathons was that the only real arbiter of how well you did was your time. People ask, 'What time did you run?' There really isn't anything else left to ask. Here, you can ask, 'What did you think of the burning obstacle?'"[12]

Even if you're not into running through burning hay bales or sliding headfirst into a pond that one blogger described as smelling like "a thousand years of fermented goose poop,"[13] experiential purchases make better stories than material purchases. When researchers at Cornell University asked pairs of strangers to discuss purchases made with the intent to increase their happiness, those who talked about experiential purchases enjoyed the conversation more.[14] They even liked their partner more than those who exchanged stories about material purchases. Individuals who prioritize experiential purchases are seen as open-minded, intelligent, and outgoing.

Like diving into fermented goose poop, experiential purchases not only provide us with entertaining anecdotes, but also add texture to our broader life stories. When undergraduates wrote a summary of their "life story" (at the tender age of approximately 19), they were more likely to mention experiential purchases, rather than material goods.[15] In a follow-up study conducted at a Chicago museum, people ranging in age from 18 to 72 reported that someone who knew of their experiential purchases (and nothing else) would have a clearer window into their "true, essential self" than someone with knowledge of only their material purchases. The self-defining nature of experiences can be seen in the pictures that people draw of themselves and their purchases (Figure 1). Traveling through Budapest or Africa, going to the prom, and seeing a Broadway show—experiences like these are the purchases that reflect who we are. Such defining experiences provide more happiness than designer purses and Swiss watches.

The Experiential CV

In the Oscar-winning film *Eternal Sunshine of the Spotless Mind*, Jim Carrey and Kate Winslet play a couple who have split up and hired a company called Lacuna to remove all traces of each other from their memories. It seems like a good idea—not only out of sight, but out of mind. As the movie progresses, however, they begin to recognize the emotional value of their memories. Losing their memories means losing themselves.

Figure 1. Diagramming the Self

Travis Carter and Tom Gilovich asked students at Cornell University to think of four material purchases and four experiential purchases they had made. Then students were presented with a circle representing the self and were asked to draw circles for each of their purchases to indicate how closely linked each purchase was to their sense of self. Here are the diagrams drawn by three of the students in the study. Experiential purchases are shaded in gray.

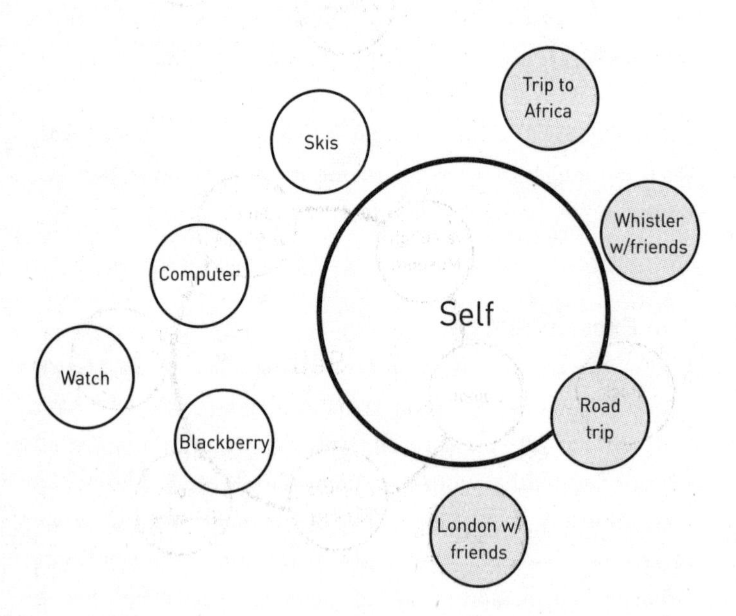

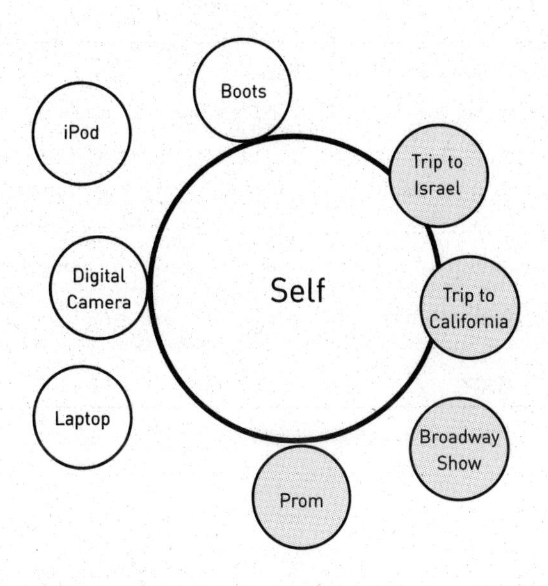
Boots
iPod
Trip to
Israel
Digital
Camera
Self
Trip to
California
Laptop
Broadway
Show
Prom

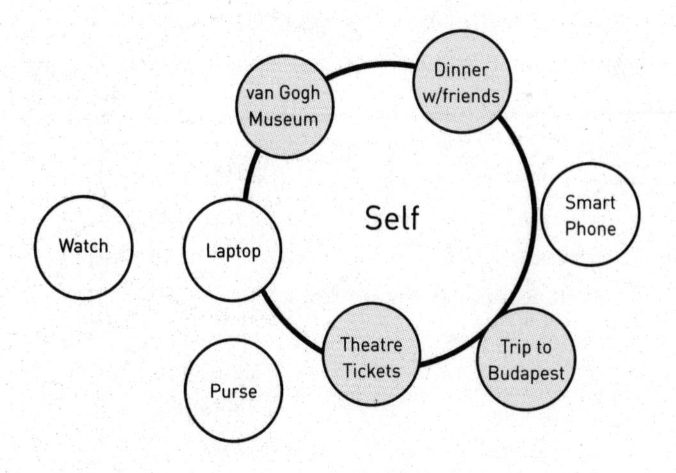
Dinner
w/friends
van Gogh
Museum
Smart
Phone
Self
Watch
Laptop
Theatre
Tickets
Trip to
Budapest
Purse

In a study that, oddly enough, appears loosely based on the movie, participants recalled either an important experiential or material purchase, and then read the following:

> Imagine that you could go back in time for just an instant, and make a different decision, choosing one of the alternatives instead, and then come back to the present. All of your current memories of that purchase would be replaced with new memories that were formed as a result of the different choice, but ultimately you have arrived back at the same time and place, right where you are now.

Faced with this proposition, the individuals who looked back on an experiential purchase were much less willing to trade in their memories for new ones, helping to explain why they found these purchases so satisfying.[16]

Futuristic pharmacology aside, people will go to great lengths to protect their most valuable memories. Think about an evening out that was particularly special for you (perhaps your first date with the person you married) and another evening that was pleasant, but not particularly special. Would you be willing to go back to the same place you visited on each of those evenings—but with someone else? Faced with this question, more than 10 percent of respondents said that there were *no circumstances* in which they would be willing to return to the scene of their special evening with a different person (whereas just 2 percent felt this way about their pleasant, but less special evening).[17] One man described a special evening during his honeymoon, explaining that he feared going back to that place because of the risk of having "a poor experience that taints our memory."

Reflecting on such special past experiences can provoke feelings of nostalgia. Defined as "a sentimental longing for the past," this emotion was first characterized as a "cerebral disease" in the 1600s by a Swiss physician, based on his examination of soldiers fighting far from home.[18] But modern research paints a different picture of nostalgia, suggesting that it provides a kind of existential resource. When people feel a sense of meaninglessness, nostalgia provides a shield against diminished well-being, bolstering vitality and reducing stress.[19] As sociologist Fred Davis puts it, nostalgia "reassures us of past happiness and accomplishment; and since these still remain on deposit, as it were, in the bank of our memory, it simultaneously bestows upon us a certain worth."[20]

Sweden's Ice Hotel lies some 125 miles north of the Arctic Circle. Visitors sleep on beds made of ice, with ambient temperatures of minus five degrees Celsius. This place is *cold.* While the average Travelodge offers a more comfortable sleeping experience, spending a night at the Ice Hotel serves a different purpose for visitors: it builds their "experiential CV."[21] In response to the demand for unusual and memorable experiences that enrich people's life stories, Finland now offers visitors an entire village made of ice and snow. And ice hotels are popping up in chilly climes from Romania to Quebec. Asked whether they would prefer to stay in Quebec City's ice hotel (the Hôtel de Glace) or a more standard Marriott hotel in Florida, the vast majority of respondents thought that the Florida hotel would be more pleasant.[22] But almost all of them thought the ice hotel would be more *memorable.* And memorability won the day, with 72 percent indicating that given a choice of where to stay, they'd ice it up.

Collecting memorable experiences, even at the expense of

momentary enjoyment, seems to hold particular appeal for individuals who care about using their time productively—those people who can't even spend five minutes waiting for a train without reaching for their smartphones. If you want to know whether your new girlfriend would rather stay at a beachfront Marriott or an ice hotel, take a look at her wristwatch. If her watch is slow, she's more likely to prefer the Marriott; if it's fast, she's more likely to prefer the ice hotel. When visitors to New York's Central Park were presented with this choice, more than 70 percent of people with slow watches chose the Marriott, while more than 70 percent of people with fast watches chose the ice hotel.* For people whose watches are always running a few minutes fast, unpleasantness may even be desirable if it contributes a compelling line to their experiential CV.

In defense of beachfront Marriotts everywhere, we hasten to add that it's possible to take the pursuit of collectable experiences too far. Liz learned this lesson after agreeing to rent a campervan for a Canadian road trip with a group of men whose girlfriends were supposed to come, but wisely bailed. The goal: swimming in the Arctic Ocean. As it turns out, the Arctic is really far away. After days and days of driving through the barren landscape, devoid of other human contact, "Blackwater Liz"—as she had come to be known—spent hours at a pay phone, trying to book a flight back home. She failed, and is now married to one of those men. The relentless quest for novel, memorable experiences

* Of course, it's possible that people who chose the ice hotel might be happier basking in the sunshine at the beachfront Marriot. Research shows that people don't always choose the option they would enjoy the most. Scoping out wristwatches helps us predict what others will *choose*, not necessarily what they will *enjoy*.

often necessitates the use of annoying phrases such as "What doesn't kill you makes you stronger," or as the Roman philosopher Seneca put it, "Things that were hard to bear are sweet to remember."[23]

Seneca had a point. There is some evidence that even rather unpleasant experiences can become rosier in the kaleidoscope of memory.[24] In a classic study, researchers tagged along with a group of students on a three-week bicycle trip through California.[25] The trip did not go smoothly. There were mosquitoes. It rained a lot. During the trip, 61 percent of the students reported feeling disappointed with it. Yet after the trip, only 11 percent reported disappointment. As one cyclist put it, "All of the complaining that I did seems so silly to me now, because all I can remember is making a lot of great friends."

This is not to say that all negativity evaporates from our memories. Particularly negative experiences can sometimes become magnified in memory's rearview mirror.[26] After Liz's arctic road trip, none of the travelers forgot the image of the campervan's waste disposal system springing a leak, creating a flood of black water (and now you can guess the origins of Liz's nickname). But because experiences often elude easy comparisons, experiential purchases seem to inoculate us against the pernicious negative emotion of regret. As researchers Travis Carter and Tom Gilovich explain, "It is a relatively straightforward task to align the size, picture quality and cost of several televisions before deciding which has the best combination of features. Choosing a dessert by comparing the taste and texture of an apple tart to that of an orange sorbet is considerably more difficult; one must literally compare apples to oranges."[27]

After buying an HTC smartphone recently, Liz's husband was plagued by an irresistible urge to compare his phone to the phalanx of iPhones surrounding him. At parties, he'd query friends about battery life and screen brightness. He is not alone in his anxiety about having purchased an inferior product. Across major and mundane purchases alike, people are much more likely to experience buyer's remorse for material goods.[28]

This idea is not lost on innovative businesses. To sell tickets for its upcoming spaceflights, Virgin Galactic filled a beautiful brochure with striking photos of the earth from space and futuristic images of suborbital travel. In contrast, the cover is a simple gray, splashed with the words of Mark Twain: "Twenty years from now you will be more disappointed by the things that you didn't do than by the ones you did do." This marketing strategy is clever. If you want people to put down a $20,000 deposit for something that doesn't exist yet, you better convince them that they won't regret it. But it also turns out to be true. Looking back on their past decisions about whether to purchase experiences, 83 percent of people sided with Mark Twain, reporting that their biggest single regret was one of *inaction*, of passing up the chance to buy an experience when the opportunity came along. The opposite was true for material goods; most people's biggest regret was buying something that they wish they hadn't.

The apples-and-oranges quality of experiences also makes it easier to enjoy them in the moment, unfettered by depressing comparisons. Researchers at Cornell gave students a Pilot G2 Super Fine pen as a prize and asked them to try it out.[29] When it was surrounded by inferior prizes, including an unsharpened pencil and a bag of rubber bands, the students gave the pen rave reviews. Other students saw the same pen alongside a USB drive and a leather-bound notebook. The presence of more desirable goods significantly diminished the pen's appeal. This simple study illustrates one of the major barriers to increasing human well-being. We are happy with things, until we find out there are better things available.

Luckily, this tendency may be limited to *things*. Even the simplest experiences, like eating a bag of crisps, are relatively immune to the detrimental effects of attractive alternatives. Offered the chance to eat a bag of crisps, students enjoyed the crisps' crunchy goodness regardless of whether the surrounding alternatives included Cadbury's chocolate or clam juice.

Making the Most of Every Strawberry

The distinction between material and experiential purchases isn't quite as clear as we've been making it. Crisps seem more experiential than pens, sure, but we hope few people would list "eating crisps" as a life-defining experience. While a trip to Paris is clearly an experience and a painting of Paris is clearly a material thing, a mélange of other purchases fall somewhere in the hazy middle. Is this book a material thing or an experience? If you bought this book for its decorative cover to adorn the shelves of your living room or impress your colleagues, then it lies closer to the material end of the continuum. If you intend to read this book and then pass it along to a friend, delete it from your Kindle, or toss it in a raging fire, it falls on the experiential side. Although we're not advocating book burning, the evidence suggests that you might be less likely to regret buying it if you view it as an experiential purchase.[30]

Just shifting your focus can alter whether a purchase feels like an experience. Imagine buying a boxed set of music by your favorite band. Think about where you would put it in your house and how it would fit with the rest of your collection. Now forget that, and consider instead how you would feel while listening to these songs, focusing on your connection with the music. Research shows that people are more likely to see the boxed set of music as an experiential purchase when they follow the second set of instructions.[31] This mental flexibility provides a springboard to greater satisfaction with whatever we buy.

Businesses have capitalized on this idea through efforts to make their products more experiential. Consider the humble strawberry. Given the limited shelf life of berries, it is clearly an experiential good. But in the hands of Ferran Adrià, one of the world's top chefs, the strawberry becomes an *Experience.* When Mike had the opportunity to dine at Adrià's restaurant elBulli shortly before it closed in 2011, he was disgruntled that one course consisted of nothing more than a strawberry. But when he bit into the strawberry, he tasted gin and tonic. And then barbecue sauce. And finally, the strawberry. Adrià designed this culinary experiment to evoke the experience of a summer barbecue, attempting to bring back nostalgic memories by activating what he calls our sixth sense. The renowned chef says his goal is to turn "eating into an experience that supersedes eating."[32] Each year Adrià completely re-created the menu, so every diner knew that he or she had a dining experience that could never be repeated.

But the elBulli experience extends beyond the food itself. Even the mundane act of getting a reservation was part of the experience. Before shutting its doors, elBulli often received 1–2 million reservation requests per year, yet served just 8,000 customers. Some diners tried for years to get a spot. As a young Parisian woman named Clotilde Dusoulier wrote on her food blog, "I remember the yearning, and I remember the pang that followed closely: considering the small number of guests that the restaurant could accommodate each season, the dream seemed out of reach."[33] Even getting to elBulli was an experience, involving a two-hour car ride from Barcelona via a curvy road with poor or absent signage up a mountain. The restaurant invited storytelling on a grand scale: bloggers have written volumes about their experiences at elBulli, often accompanied by sensual images of each dish, satisfying the Internet demand for food porn. When elBulli comes up, no matter what company Mike is in, there are always several people who request—no, *demand*—a blow-by-blow recounting of his experience.

After achieving her dream of dining at elBulli, Clotilde recounted the experience on her blog in scintillating detail: "It took us six hours to go through the entire meal—from 8pm to 2am—but we were in such a state of elation that it was hard to tell if it had been two minutes or two days since we had first sat down. Dining at elBulli is certainly a one-of-a-kind experience, and I wish it upon anyone who's passionate about food, who has broad tastes, who is tickled by the discovery of new flavors, and who is happy to be whisked away on a flying carpet driven by a mad scientist, even if the ride leaves him a bit dizzy."[34]

While it may seem unlikely that dining at elBulli would have much in common with a trip to space, our conversations with Virgin Galactic astronauts revealed similar themes. Did Marcia consider buying something *instead* of a flight into space with the life insurance money? "Not in the slightest," she said. The singularity of this experience makes it impossible to compare it to anything else. In addition, Virgin Galactic has taken steps to create a community of astronauts, throwing parties and organizing meet-ups to watch launches. And of course, experiences can be shared with family and friends. Even though Marcia will not go into space with John as they had dreamed, she told us that her friends and family are anticipating the trip along with her. "It's not just me—it's a whole bunch of people going with me," she said.

Understanding why experiences provide more happiness than material goods can also help us to choose the most satisfying *kinds* of experiences. The specific experiences that people enjoy vary with their age, gender, personality, and a zillion idiosyncratic characteristics. Liz's ideal holiday, for example, would involve surfing a different Nicaraguan beach every day. Mike's would entail surfing couches for his afternoon naps. But our discussion so far suggests that across a wide range of different types of experiences, you're likely to get the biggest bang for your buck if:

- The experience brings you together with other people, fostering a sense of social connection.
- The experience makes a memorable story that you'll enjoy retelling for years to come.
- The experience is tightly linked to your sense of who you are or want to be.
- The experience provides a unique opportunity, eluding easy comparison with other available options.

Equally interesting is what *doesn't* matter. A trip into space might have a bigger impact on happiness than buying that Tudor-style house, but $200,000 is a lot to pay for just six minutes in space. Remarkably, though, the length of an experience has little impact on the pleasure people remember deriving from it.[35] Perhaps Jemaine Clement from Flight of the Conchords was on to something when he sang in "Business Time" that "when it's with me you only need two minutes." Why? "Because I'm so intense." In a New Zealand study, holiday-makers rated their happiness on each day of their trip via text message.[36] One to two weeks after they got back, they reported their overall feelings about the holiday. Although the holidays ranged in length from four to fourteen days, the duration of the trip had no bearing on their overall feelings about the trip. The text messages revealed that holiday-makers felt happier during their trip than they did in their daily lives. But after the trip, they remembered feeling even better than they actually had. And the worst part of the trip failed to drag down their overall evaluations of the experience. It may be worth paying for an experience that meets the four criteria above, even if it won't last long and there's some risk of unpleasantness along the way.

Resisting the Lure of the Rubber Frog

Google used to give its top employees monetary awards as high as seven figures. "But we've moved away from them," explains Laszlo Bock, the company's senior vice president for people operations.[37] Google's research reveals that large cash-based or stock-based awards can be divisive. And Laszlo says, "They're just not as meaningful as a life experience." Google redesigned the award to provide a compelling life experience for its most exceptional managers. One year, the winners traveled through Costa Rica along with their spouses and members of senior management. "The experience that they have on the trip—with one another, across the company—is far more powerful and valuable to them than if we'd given them the cash value, or even ten times the cash value," Laszlo explains. "And it has a much bigger impact on the broader organization."

Providing experiences instead of more traditional material things can help to attract and retain customers and employees. And the idea is gaining traction in even the ultimate outpost of materialism: the wedding registry. A company called Traveler's Joy is working to move beyond the standard registry for a soon-to-be-married couple: that long list of products, most of which they will never use (a mandoline? a *meatball shaper*?). Using Traveler's Joy, Mike bought bullfight tickets for his newlywed friends as part of their dream holiday to Spain. A similar alternative wedding registry service, ehoneymoon registry.com, depicts a photo of a couple exploring the canals of Venice, with the tagline, "Because you don't need another toaster." On an abstract level, this message resonates with many couples. And yet it can be hard not to get sucked in by the concrete features of high-end toasters such as Cuisinart's top-rated "Total Touch" toaster, which promises to toast whole bagels and even muffins perfectly every time. Material purchases offer clear, concrete benefits, explaining their appeal. We can see them in front of us and hold them in our hands.

The benefits of experiential purchases are often more abstract. The Funky Monkey, one of the obstacles in a typical Tough Mudder race, entails crossing a set of monkey bars, randomly greased with butter, over a pit of ice-cold mud and water. On a concrete level, this experience doesn't seem like the kind of thing that a mentally healthy human being would *pay* to undertake. But considered more abstractly, completing the Funky Monkey may provide enormous value. After completing a Tough Mudder event, Trevor Bobb wrote on the company's Facebook wall, "It means much more than just finishing a race. I had shoulder surgery over a year ago and the doctor completely destroyed my shoulder. I didn't have use of my right arm for a year. Long story short, I completed all of the obstacles, and after getting across the monkey bars, my girlfriend started to cry because of what that meant for me."

Because the benefits of experiences are often more abstract than the benefits of material goods, it's easier to appreciate the value of experiential purchases with the psychological distance that time provides. Contemplating the distant future is a little like viewing the earth from space. We see the oceans and the sweeping forests, but not the tributaries and trees. As a result, we are more likely to think in abstract terms when making decisions about the distant future than the immediate future.[38] After all, dealing with an impending experience requires that we focus on the concrete details. In approaching the Funky Monkey, Trevor Bobb needed to pay attention to which bars were covered in grease, rather than thinking about how the obstacle fit in with his broader life story. And immediately after his crossing, the feeling of the slippery bars against his cold, muddy hands may have stood out more than the deeper meaning of his achievement. Indeed, research shows that satisfaction with experiential purchases tends to increase with the passage of time, while satisfaction with material purchases tends to decrease. As a respondent in one study put it, "Material possessions, they sort of become part of the background; experiences just get better with time."[39] Likewise, experiential purchases seem more appealing when people consider what to buy in a year rather than what to buy tomorrow.[40]

In the heat of the moment, however, the lure of material goods may win the day. This idea is likely familiar to any parent who has attended a birthday party at Chuck E. Cheese. At this play emporium, kids are given a cup full of tokens and set loose in a microcosmic economy where they can choose to buy experiences, like straddling a motorcycle for a race through Paris or shooting aliens with a giant gun. Alternatively, they can drop their tokens into games of chance—basically, slot machines with training wheels. These games are over in an instant and don't provide the thrill of a good, clean alien shoot-out, but they do provide something strangely addictive that the experiential games don't: tickets. Toss a token in, and a moment later, a long string of tickets comes shooting out, which can then be traded for a variety of material goods, from erasers to rubber animals. According to Steve Stroessner, father of two children, ages eight and thirteen, "The tickets are like crack." Kids will often forgo the pleasure of more experiential games to harvest them. Cami Johnson, another Chuck E. Cheese veteran, explains, "The rubber frog will fall on the floor of the car on the way home and get covered in dog hair and crumbs, and the eraser will be lost in the bottom of the backpack. While you have a permanent token of your time and labor, that permanent token is actually pretty worthless."

We don't wish to deny that material things can provide

immediate delight. There's something about the rubber bird in the hand, after all. But this material rush will likely fade, whereas the experiential high lasts much longer. Next time you reach for your wallet to buy a metaphorical rubber frog, don't let the lure of the material induce you to forgo all the happiness benefits of the experiential.

2

Make It a Treat

Sarah Silverman loves pot, porn, and fart jokes. But when it comes to indulging in these finer pleasures, the comic and former *Saturday Night Live* writer has a mantra: "Make it a treat." This epiphany came to her in the midst of her first year at New York University, when a friend found her in the midst of an extended pot bender and imparted some guru-like wisdom: "If you want to enjoy these things—things like weed—you have to make it a treat."[1] On her show, *The Sarah Silverman Program*, she puts this mantra into action by insisting that her writers temper their innate overreliance on fart jokes.

"Fart jokes make me happier than just about anything in the universe," she explains. "And for that reason I'm terrified by the idea that someday I might have had enough of them. If they are a genuine treat and a surprise, they are the surest way to send me into tear-soaked convulsions of laughter." While all of us may not share Sarah Silverman's humor preferences, her kernel of wisdom—let's call it Silverman's Mantra—extends beyond fart jokes. And it can help people make wiser spending decisions. Abundance, it turns out, is the enemy of appreciation.

Many of us are lucky enough to live in a society where chocolate is available in every supermarket, petrol station, and cinema. Ironically, though, this abundance may undermine our enjoyment of it. One afternoon, students came into a psychology lab to complete a simple task: eating a piece of chocolate.[2] The following week they returned for a second piece. Overall, the students enjoyed the chocolate less the second time than they had the first. This is the sad reality of the human experience: in general, the more we're exposed to something, the more its impact diminishes.

It's not all bad news. Getting used to things can be handy when it comes to cold winters or unpleasant smells. Early one Friday evening, Liz's Welsh corgi got sprayed by a skunk. In a moment of naïve gallantry, she scooped the stinking dog into her arms, thereby covering herself in the scent, too. After hours of bathing both herself and the dog in tomatoes and other home remedies, Liz found that the scent had faded. She gave the dog a Snausage and headed off to a friend's party. Moments after Liz's arrival, the party hostess nervously sniffed the air and exclaimed, "Skunk!" The cure that Liz believed the home remedies had wrought was due to her own olfactory fatigue. After prolonged exposure to the bad smell, Liz became habituated to it, and its pungency faded. Many of us have experienced the process of getting used to bad things. We often fail to realize that a similar kind of habituation can kick in for positive experiences, like buying shiny new toys. From chocolate bars to luxury cars, habituation represents a fundamental barrier to deriving lasting pleasure from our purchases.

Like houses, cars are among the largest purchases that most people make. Is it best to splurge on a BMW, economize with a Ford Escort, or settle for the mid-level option of a Honda Accord? When researchers at the University of Michigan asked students to *predict* how much pleasure they would experience while driving each type of car, the BMW was the clear winner.[3] But do drivers experience more happiness behind the wheel of an expensive car? To find out, the Michigan researchers asked car owners to think back on the last time they had driven their car, rating how much they enjoyed that drive. Although their cars ranged widely in value, from around $400 to $40,000, there was no relationship at all between the market value of the car and the amount of enjoyment the owners got from driving it that day.

But here's the twist in the road: The researchers asked other drivers to list their car's make, model, and year, and then consider how they typically felt while driving it. When car owners thought about their vehicles in this light, those who owned more expensive cars reported deriving more enjoyment from driving. Suddenly there was a relationship between a car's value and its emotional payoff. Why? When people are asked how something *generally* makes them feel, they tend to draw on equally general theories to form an answer. Rather than reconstructing how they felt each of the last fifty times they drove the Bimmer and then averaging these experiences, a BMW owner is likely to think something like, "I own a midnight blue Z4 with three hundred horsepower and a retractable hardtop. Of course I enjoy driving it. Next question." These undeniably fabulous features are likely to make a big difference for enjoyment during an initial test drive, which is why smart salespeople focus our attention on these features at the time of purchase. Novelty attracts the spotlight of attention, focusing our minds and exciting our emotions. But once we get used to something—even something as nice as a midnight blue Z4—the spotlight moves on. Driving to the grocery shop in the dead of winter, we think about being stuck in the left lane behind an octogenarian in an Oldsmobile, about whether the shop will have any hot rotisserie chickens left, about almost anything *other* than the make and model of the car we're driving. Retractable hardtops just aren't that relevant in subzero temperatures. And this explains why driving a more expensive car doesn't usually provide more joy than driving an economy model.

Unless, that is, we make driving a treat. In a final study, the Michigan researchers asked car owners to think about the last time they had driven their car just for fun. When people thought back on their most recent joy ride, individuals with more expensive cars reported more pleasure from driving. But these joy rides were remarkably rare. So, driving a BMW probably won't provide you with any more pleasure than driving a Ford Escort—except on those rare occasions when your attention turns to the car itself, whether directed by a question from a researcher or a joy ride on a winding mountain road.

The Deceptive Simplicity of Silverman's Mantra

According to Oprah Winfrey, "The single greatest thing you can do to change your life today would be to start being grateful for what you have."[4] This is good advice. But, like a grapefruit diet, adopting an attitude of gratitude is easy at first but quickly becomes almost impossible. Because novelty captures our attention, we feel buoyantly grateful for things that catch us by surprise.[5] The seventeen-year-old who lives out the teenage fantasy of discovering a new car wrapped in a giant red bow on his birthday will no doubt experience a surge of joy and gratitude. But these feelings are likely to fade as being a car owner becomes just another part of his daily experience and identity.

Following Oprah's advice is hard for all of us, and ironically, it gets even harder as people edge closer and closer to Oprah's end of the wealth spectrum. In a study of working adults in Belgium, wealthier individuals reported a lower proclivity to savor life's little pleasures. They were less likely to say that they would pause to appreciate a beautiful waterfall on a hike, or stay present in the moment during a romantic weekend getaway.[6] This phenomenon helps explain why the relationship between income and happiness is weaker than many people expect. At the same time that money increases our happiness by giving us access to all kinds of wonderful things, *knowing* we have access to wonderful things undermines our happiness by reducing our tendency to appreciate life's small joys.

Just thinking about money can produce some of the same detrimental effects as having a lot of it. If you ever want those around you to act like wealthy people for a few minutes, research suggests that all you have to do is show them a photograph of a big stack of money.[7] Seeing this photograph makes people less inclined to linger by a waterfall or savor life's other little pleasures, just like individuals who actually *have* a lot of money.[8]

The idea that wealth interferes with the proclivity to savor echoes the theme of the classic 1964 children's book *Charlie and the Chocolate Factory*. The young hero, Charlie Bucket, lives in a tiny two-room house with one bed and four grandparents. While the wealthier kids in the story gorge themselves on a plentiful supply of chocolate bars, Charlie's family saves up just enough money to give him one chocolate bar a year, on his birthday. Each time, he would "treasure it as though it were a bar of solid gold," spending days just looking at it before he would finally "peel back a *tiny* bit of the paper wrapping at one corner to expose a *tiny* bit of chocolate, and then he would take a *tiny* nibble, just enough to allow the lovely sweet taste to spread out slowly over his tongue. The next day, he would take another tiny nibble, and so on," making his annual bar of chocolate last over a month.[9]

In a Willy Wonkaesque study, Canadian students saw a photograph of money and then ate a piece of chocolate, as researchers surreptitiously observed them.[10] Compared to others who hadn't seen the money, students who saw this photograph spent substantially less time eating their chocolate, chowing it down like Augustus Gloop. The observers also noted less enjoyment on their faces. Because even a simple reminder of wealth undermines our ability to enjoy life's little treats, living by Silverman's Mantra may not be easy, at least for those of us who are wealthier than Charlie Bucket. According to Silverman: "That's why mantras need to be repeated—they're fucking hard to remember."[11]

Most people recognize that they won't appreciate their car quite as much after owning it for twenty-four months as they did when they first drove it home, just as the twenty-fourth fart joke won't be as funny as the first one. When researchers at Yale asked people to predict how their enjoyment of various products might change over time, the majority expected their enjoyment would decline, for products ranging from a plasma TV to a kaleidoscope.[12] The problem is that it's easy to lose sight of this knowledge when a shiny new toy is right at your fingertips. In another study, the Yale researchers gave students a kaleidoscope and asked half of them to predict how much they would enjoy playing with it a week later. Others predicted how much they would enjoy it a day later.[13] Students expected to enjoy the kaleidoscope just as much regardless of the time frame they considered, even though most of their peers in the previous study believed that enjoyment of a kaleidoscope would decline with time. In other words, though we understand that enjoyment often fades over time, we don't always *apply* that knowledge when contemplating a new toy. When researchers prompt people to consider the passage of time, this reminder triggers the correct belief that the tide of enjoyment quickly recedes. In the absence of such reminders, however, people envision an unchanging sea of pleasure. As a result, products often provide less lasting enjoyment than people expect. Indeed, after students took their kaleidoscopes home, they reported enjoying the toys much less if they were contacted a week later rather than a day later.

This drop in enjoyment occurs because people are fundamentally different from thermometers. Put a thermometer in lukewarm water, and the mercury rises to reflect the water's precise temperature. "It does not matter whether the mercury was previously stored in an oven or an ice bath, or whether it was stored in either place for hours or days or years," researchers Shane Frederick and George Loewenstein explain. "Mercury has no memory for previous states. Humans and other organisms do not behave this way."[14] Stick your hand in lukewarm water and it may feel piping hot if you've just come inside on a frigid winter morning, but cool and refreshing on a sweaty summer afternoon. Leave your hand in the water and the intensity of the initial sensation will soon subside. Our emotional system works in much the same way, making us highly sensitive to change. Understanding this fundamental difference between the thermometer and what we might call the "cheerometer" enables us to develop specific spending strategies designed to combat ennui.

The Wisdom of Candy Corn

Because we lack mercury's amnesia, our enjoyment of a piece of chocolate typically declines from one week to the next. But there's a way to maximize the pleasure of that second confection. Temporarily giving up chocolate can restore our ability to enjoy it. After an initial chocolate tasting, students promised to abstain from chocolate for one week.[15] Another group of students pledged to eat as much chocolate as they comfortably could, and they received a two-pound bag of chocolate to help them fulfill their pledge. The students who left with this reservoir of chocolatey goodness may seem like the lucky ones. But their sweet windfall came at a price. When they returned the following week to sample additional chocolate, they enjoyed it much less than they had the week before. People only enjoyed chocolate as much the second week as they had the first if they had given it up in between.*

If abundance is the enemy of appreciation, scarcity may be our best ally. As it turns out, all of Mike's favorite treats are widely available for just a brief period each year: Red Hots (easiest to find in February), candy corn (October), plus peppermint stick ice cream and eggnog (December). Because he takes long breaks from these treats during the summer months, he's happy all over again when October rolls around and the candy corn starts flowing.

Giving up Red Hots and candy corn can provide an escape hatch from adaptation, helping turn our favorite things back into treats. But we are not advocating austerity, though the

* It's possible that people felt dejected during the week they gave up chocolate, perhaps offsetting the pleasure they experienced when they got to have it again. But everyone also reported how they felt each day during the week between chocolate tastings, and there was little evidence of diminished happiness among those who gave up chocolate.

simple life does have its adherents. In the name of voluntary simplicity, people on the "Great American Apparel Diet" have given up buying clothes for a year.[16] Other individuals have stripped their monthly wardrobes down to just six items.[17] As coworkers in nearby cubicles might attest, it is possible to take this strategy too far. Although a quick Google search reveals no end of claims about the benefits of voluntary simplicity, there is little rigorous evidence that emptying your life of worldly possessions results in a Zen-like state of pure bliss.

When Kristen Martini was in her mid-thirties, she moved from a large suburban home to a tiny cottage in the woods, taking only some food, a bit of clothing, and her two children, and leaving behind the enviable trappings of her comfortable life.[18] The values and goals that prompted this move—placing personal growth and fulfillment above image and financial success—are indeed strongly linked to happiness. People who describe themselves as voluntary simplifiers do report greater happiness.[19] But their happiness appears to stem more from the values and mind-sets associated with voluntary simplicity than from major lifestyle changes. In other words, profound self-denial may be overrated.

Instead, we stress the importance of *treats.* Liz used to have a latte every day. At first the latte was a treat, especially as a post-grad student, when it represented a substantial portion of her daily budget. But while rushing to work one day, chugging her latte to ingest a sufficient amount of caffeine before a meeting, she realized that the latte was no longer a treat. She switched her daily drink to the regular brewed coffee that everyone drank before the age of espresso, cutting her coffee budget dramatically. Every so often, though, she decides,

"Today is a latte day." She heads to a coffee shop, orders a latte, and savors the foamy goodness anew.

While there is no convincing evidence that *reducing* consumption provides a panacea for increasing happiness, a growing body of research suggests that *altering* consumption patterns can provide a route to getting more happiness for less money. And as we'll see in the rest of the chapter, even seemingly trivial changes can make a big difference.

Living the Portuguese Dream

Jaime Kurtz, a social psychologist and dog lover, has a longstanding dream: to create puppies that stay puppies forever. Ironically, her own research (thankfully not in genetic engineering) suggests that this is a bad idea. As Jaime's research demonstrates, when we know something won't last forever, we're more likely to savor it. When students feel that the end of their undergraduate experience is near, they savor their remaining time by taking the scenic route to class, snapping photos, and visiting their favorite places and classmates.[20]

Knowing that something won't last forever can make us appreciate it more. For adults in their sunset years, that "something" becomes life itself. While young people seek abundance, older adults engage in a kind of pruning process, trimming away the people and things that don't deliver an emotional payoff.[21] In 1995, at the age of 120, a Frenchwoman named Jeanne Calment officially became the oldest person ever. When a *Newsweek* reporter asked her about the sort of future she envisioned for herself, the super-centenarian replied, "A very short one."[22] Recognizing that an end is near holds a key to happiness, helping us turn readily available comforts back into treats.

This idea also helps to explain an enduring puzzle of forgone pleasure: Why don't people get around to visiting famous landmarks in their own hometown? After living in London for a whole year, residents typically report that they've visited fewer landmarks—from Big Ben to Kensington Palace—than visitors who have only been there for two weeks.[23] Although London attracts more international visitors than any other city in the world,[24] most London residents report having visited more landmarks in cities other than their own. Only when they themselves are about to move away, or when out-of-town guests come to visit, do they seek out the sights of their own city. When people get around to visiting their hometown landmarks, they report enjoying the experience. The trouble is that when a pleasurable activity is always available, we may never get around to doing it, thereby missing out on a relatively inexpensive source of happiness.

The Big Ben Problem suggests that introducing a limited time window may encourage people to seize opportunities for treats. Imagine you've just gotten a gift certificate for a piece of delicious cake and a beverage at a high-end French pastry shop. Would you rather see the gift certificate stamped with an expiration date two months from today, or just three weeks from now? Faced with this choice, most people were happier with the two-month option, and 68 percent reported that they would use it before this expiration date.[25] But when they received a gift certificate for a tasty pastry at a local shop, only 6 percent of people redeemed it when they were given a two-month expiration date, compared to 31 percent of people who were given the shorter three-week window. People given two months to redeem the certificate kept thinking they could do it later, creating another instance of the Big Ben Problem—and leading them to miss out on a delicious treat. Several years ago, electronics chain Best Buy reported gaining $43 million from gift certificates that went unredeemed,[26] propelling some consumer advocates and policy makers to push for extended expiration dates. But this strategy will likely backfire. We may have more success at maximizing our happiness when treats are only available for a limited time.

In June 2011, a chorus of tweets heralded the arrival of a culinary wonder:

> @BJIT: #doubledown is coming back!!! God bless the colonel!
>
> @kevinelop: OMG!! . . . The Double Down is back at KFC!!!
>
> @iamToddyTickles: KFC's #doubledowns for Breakfast. Mmmmm. Mmmmmm. Yummmmmmy. I'm full.

Despite his precious Twitter handle, iamToddyTickles appears to be a fully grown man in his profile picture, yet his tweet echoes the slobbery exuberance of Scooby Doo. What could have prompted such an onslaught of emotion, ranging from unadulterated excitement to utter incoherence? KFC's Double Down features two slices of bacon, two kinds of cheese, and the Colonel's secret sauce, all sandwiched between two slabs of fried chicken. According to KFC, it's "so meaty, there's no room for a bun!"

This bunless "sandwich" was a hit in the United States, but in Canada, it was a sensation. The Double Down (translated for our French-Canadian friends as *Coup Double*, or "Double Punch") made KFC history, becoming the chain's best-selling new item in Canada ever.[27] When the sandwich made its Canadian debut in the fall of 2010, KFC sold a million Double Downs in less than a month, enough "to stretch across 2,083 hockey rinks," according to the company's press release.[28] (For readers unfamiliar with Canadian culture, all Canadian measurements are in hockey rink units, or HRUs.) Social media activity was intense, and consumers even organized Double Down "Bro Downs" where men competed to see who could guzzle the most Double Downs.

In response to the initial runaway success of its product, KFC pulled the sandwich off the menu across most of Canada. This move may seem strange in an industry where a pivotal goal—in the words of Coca-Cola's long-standing mantra—is to be "within an arm's reach of desire."[29] According to KFC Canada's chief marketing officer, David Vivenes, KFC is about "making moments that are so good." But by removing the Double Down from the menu, KFC made the moment when it came back in 2011 not just "so good," but even better. Nor is KFC alone in adopting this approach. McDonald's has pursued a similar strategy with its McRib sandwich, a ground pork patty with barbecue sauce, onions, and pickles. Although pork supplies are steady, the McRib has been continually taken off the market and reintroduced—always for a limited time—over the past three decades. Ashlee Yingling, of McDonald's media relations department, explained that the company makes the McRib available in the fall, thereby creating nostalgia for summer barbecues.[30]

The consumer response has been obsession. If you live in the U.S., and want to know when and where you might get your hands on a McRib, you can visit McRib fan Alan Klein's "McRib Locator" website (http://kleincast.com/maps/mcrib.php), a map with a comprehensive list of confirmed, possible, and questionable McRib sightings. McDonald's kicked off its latest McRib launch with a "Legends of the McRib" event in New York City. The McRib was a key contributor to a 4.8 percent increase in company sales in November 2010.[31]

Long before innovations like bunless sandwiches and boneless ribs, Disney began harnessing the power of limited availability by making its movies available for limited periods.[32] The company locks away *Dumbo*, *Cinderella*, *Peter Pan*, and other hits in the "Disney vault," where they remain unavailable for years at a time. Like Cinderella herself, these movies rush out of the ball while the party's still going strong, before the magic wears off. Many other companies adopted similar strategies, and the psychologist Robert Cialdini devotes an entire chapter of his classic book *Influence* to the creative and downright crafty ways in which scarcity has been used to move product. Although Cialdini admits to a "grudging admiration for the practitioners who made this simple device work in a multitude of ways,"[33] he urges readers to resist the lure of scarcity marketing, coaching them on "how to say no."[34] If we take Silverman's mantra and the science behind it seriously, however, scarcity marketing starts to look like a win-win. That is, people may savor everything from the Double Down to *Dumbo* more when they know these delights won't be available forever, increasing their own satisfaction even as companies ring up increased sales.

Applying this principle is straightforward when it comes to ephemeral delights such as movies and bunless sandwiches. But what about major purchases? Derek Lee is an aspiring actor and filmmaker who owns a beautiful, bright red Mini Cooper. If you owned a sporty little car, you might be tempted to drive it all the time, settling in to the comfy leather seats whenever you needed to get groceries or meet friends for dinner. But Derek lives in Vancouver, Canada, where public transit is excellent and car insurance is expensive. So, when Derek first got the Mini Cooper, he kept it in the garage and insured it only on the days when he really wanted to use it, rather than paying regular monthly car insurance and using the car every time he needed to run an errand. As his mildly traumatized former passengers can attest, Derek got the most out of those days, hugging turns and accelerating through straightaways like he was auditioning for a car commercial. Recently, he decided to insure his car full-time, but now, he says, driving is "just about contained road rage and not killing people." He looks back wistfully on the earlier years, when he "drove exuberantly."

Car-sharing companies like Zipcar provide customers with a similar opportunity for exuberance by turning driving back into a treat. Whereas traditional car rental companies choose standard cars in the dullest colors of the rainbow, the first Zipcar was a tricked-out lime-green Volkswagen Beetle.[35] The founder and former CEO of Zipcar, Robin Chase, pointed to the key difference between driving your own car and driving a Zipcar: You use your own car for everything. Zipcars are for "outings." Higher-end companies, like the Classic Car Club, founded in London in 1995, take this approach to its logical extreme. For a hefty membership fee, the Classic Car Club gives members access to a "staggeringly stylish fleet of cars," including Ferraris and Maseratis.[36] In Manhattan, club members pay almost $11,000 for thirteen days of driving the club's "high-end supercars." This doesn't sound like a bargain. But the cost of actually *owning* one of these cars is mind-boggling. And we're willing to bet that members' attention stays focused on the "supercars" during those magical thirteen days, making each of those eleven thousand dollars count.

Car-sharing is now a familiar concept, but creative companies are making it possible for their clients to share ownership and access to just about everything, from villas and handbags to dogs and French truffle trees.[37] According to our favorite Portuguese saying, "You should never have a yacht; you should have a friend with a yacht." (To be honest, it's also the only Portuguese saying we know.) By joining SailTime, members can live the Portuguese dream by sharing a yacht with up to seven other people. In describing SailTime, a recent media story warned consumers that sharing the yacht means "there is no guarantee you will always be able to use it when you want."[38] This apparent limitation is precisely what helps consumers make it a treat. Limiting your access to everything from the McRib to Maseratis helps to reset your cheerometer. That is, knowing you can't have access to something all the time may help you appreciate it more when you do.

And Now for a Brief Interruption

When you love a television show—say, *Peep Show*—you might think the best way to maximize your happiness is to buy the DVD set and watch all the episodes straight through. Getting rid of the commercials and eliminating the weeklong wait between episodes seems sensible. But research suggests that taking breaks between episodes can increase your enjoyment. Perhaps most amazingly, commercials can *improve* the experience of watching television.[39] Even entertaining shows can start to drag after five to seven minutes, decreasing our enjoyment. Commercials disrupt that adaptation process, so when the show comes back on, we can fall in love with Mark and Jeremy all over again.

As you might expect, the content of the program matters. Television shows like *Lost* and *CSI*, which cut unexpectedly from one dramatic scene to another, may circumvent the need for commercials by providing built-in disruptions. For experiences that are more uniform, though, interruptions can help to "re-virginize" us, wiping our pleasure slates clean. And these interruptions may increase our overall pleasure even if the interruptions themselves are annoying. To test this idea, researchers created a mash-up of popular songs, including "Lose Yourself" by Eminem, "My Sharona" by the Knack, and "Sometimes" by Michael Norton (yes, *that* Michael Norton).[40] They created sixty-second versions of each song by taking brief samples and looping them, then played the "song" without interruption for one group of listeners. Others, however, listened to the first fifty seconds, and then heard ten seconds of irritating guitar feedback lifted from an Australian punk band. Although 99 percent of people expected to prefer the continuous song, without guitar feedback, listeners enjoyed the song more when it was disrupted. They were willing to pay more than twice as much to attend a concert by the artist compared to people who heard the continuous song.

These results create an opportunity and a puzzle for purveyors of pleasure. Take the perspective of a massage therapist. Before receiving a massage, three-quarters of people reported that they would prefer to savor the experience without interruption.[41] But those who were forced to take a break during the massage ended up enjoying it more, and were willing to pay more for their next massage. Leif Nelson and Tom Meyvis argue that "the thoughtful masseuse would maximize customer enjoyment by inserting breaks in the massage."[42] In the same breath, though, they note that this strategy comes with a catch: "Customers who are informed of the break in advance may choose to go to another, more monotonous masseuse." (Reading break: picture in your mind what a thoughtful masseuse and a monotonous masseuse might look like.)

Even the briefest of breaks can allow our cheerometers to reset. Unfortunately, resetting requires that we accept a momentary drop in pleasure. A commercial is less entertaining than any given moment of a halfway decent TV show. But that irksome GoCompare ad makes the show more enjoyable once it comes back on. Similarly, getting a backrub is better than not getting a backrub at any given point in time—but taking a break still makes the overall backrub much better.

Channeling Your Inner Tim

In the 2011 comedy *Cedar Rapids*, Ed Helms plays an insurance salesman named Tim Lippe who has never ventured outside his sleepy hometown of Brown Valley, Wisconsin. Then his company sends him to a convention in the "big city" of Cedar Rapids, Iowa. Everything about Cedar Rapids dazzles Tim, from the big buildings to the intoxicating smell of chlorine wafting up from the hotel pool. Because Tim has never traveled before, each tiny discovery provides a fresh delight.

The more people travel, the less likely they are to savor each trip. In one study, United States residents recorded how many countries they had visited and then imagined what they would do after winning a trip to three of the most common holiday destinations for Americans (California, Florida, and New York), as well as the top three "dream" destinations for

Americans (Italy, Australia, and Ireland).[43] Infrequent travelers like Tim said that they would savor the trips by expressing their excitement, talking to friends and family, getting their work done ahead of time, and looking at photos afterward. Individuals who had traveled extensively exhibited a blasé attitude toward the commonplace destinations (though they mustered some enthusiasm for the dream destinations).

Did the commonplace destinations pale in comparison to the other places the world-weary had visited? Perhaps the sunny shores of Florida fail to impress when compared to the beautiful black sand beaches of Bali. This explanation is reasonable but, as it turns out, wrong. As we saw with strawberries and space travel, experiences elude easy comparisons. Bali and Florida are like apples and oranges, and thinking of one doesn't usually trigger comparisons to the other. Rather, traveling to exotic places like Bali can change the way we see ourselves, creating a broader problem. The more countries people have visited, the more they self-identify as "world travelers." This in turn undermines their motivation to savor trips to enjoyable-but-unextraordinary destinations.

If you've been lucky enough to visit lots of places in the world, you may be destined to a lifetime of diminished savoring during visits to commonplace destinations, unless you can channel your inner Tim Lippe. In a study conducted at the Old North Church, one of the most-visited historical landmarks in Boston, American tourists completed a travel checklist just before entering the church, marking off the other cities they had visited.[44] Some tourists saw a checklist that included destinations such as New York, Orlando, and Las Vegas, places many Americans have visited. Others saw a checklist that included more exotic international destinations, such as Tokyo, Paris, and Sydney. As you'd expect, tourists checked off a lot more places when they were presented with the list of U.S. destinations, leading them to feel more well-traveled than people presented with the broader list of international destinations.

The tourists went on their way, heading inside to check out the church. But the checklist changed how they behaved when they got there. Those who saw the list of exotic international destinations entered the church feeling like they were not well-traveled, and ended up savoring their visit more. They spent significantly more time enjoying the church compared to those who saw the domestic checklist.

An app from a company called Travellerspoint enticed users with the opportunity to "plot your trips on a map to show everyone how well-travelled you are." But using this app might not be such a great idea if you want to enjoy your visits to the Old North Churches of the world. It may be better to map out all the places you'd like to visit, but haven't yet. One of the world's most revered sages—the Dalai Lama—advises us to appreciate what we do have rather than focusing on what we don't.[45] But research suggests that focusing on what we *haven't* done may trigger us to appreciate what we're doing now. Because our cheerometers lack the objectivity of mercury, the way we perceive an experience depends partly on how we perceive ourselves. And changing our sense of identity, even temporarily, can make it easier to appreciate the simple pleasure of a hotel pool.

Mating in New Pastures

As a graduate student, Liz noticed something intriguing about the behavior of her longtime boyfriend, Benjamin. When he was in a bad mood, Benjamin acted cranky around her, because he knew that Liz would put up with his unpleasant behavior. But when he bumped into a stranger or casual acquaintance, Benjamin perked right up, acting pleasant and cheerful. Because social graces forced him to abandon his own grumpiness, his bad mood often dissipated.

To understand her boyfriend's behavior, Liz invited long-term heterosexual couples into the lab. Each individual interacted either with his or her own romantic partner or with an opposite-sex stranger from another couple.[46] Just like Benjamin, people acted perky and pleasant when they interacted with strangers. And their own positive behavior enhanced their mood in a way that they failed to foresee ahead of time. Liz and her colleagues began to refer to this phenomenon as "the Benjamin Effect."

Rather than ditching your long-term romantic partner in search of a stranger, try harnessing the Benjamin Effect to improve your romantic relationship. In a follow-up study, Liz brought more couples into her lab and asked each couple to spend some time together. She told some of them to put their best face forward as they would with someone they had just met. Meanwhile, the others just had a regular old interaction with their romantic partner. People derived significantly more joy from interacting with their romantic partners when they treated the loves of their lives as though they were complete strangers.

Before writing off Valentine's Day as an excuse to sell greeting cards, remember the value of making an effort (every once in a while) to be your best self around your romantic partner. Elizabeth Haines is a forty-year-old mother of two who has been married to her husband, Terry, for more than a decade. Although Elizabeth and Terry are both working parents, they make time each week for "date night." It would be easy to flop on the couch and put in a DVD. Instead, they pay a babysitter and hit the town. "I do that kind of cougar-mom thing. You know, tight jeans, cute top, some wedge sandals. I dress as if I was going on a date," Elizabeth explains.

Elizabeth and Terry often head to a local restaurant for dinner and drinks, but her favorite date nights involve less mundane activities, like seeing a new band perform in the city. When couples do novel, exciting things together, the relationship itself feels novel and exciting. In one study, couples bound together—literally, with Velcro at their wrists and ankles—performed a series of novel physical challenges.[47] Other couples performed a duller task, slowly rolling a ball back and forth while stationed on opposite sides of a large room. Afterward, the Velcroed couples reported greater relationship satisfaction and scored higher on the Romantic Love Symptom Checklist, which includes symptoms of love such as experiencing "tingling" while thinking of the beloved.

The value of novelty emerges even in the bovine version of date night. Bulls get bored with the artificial "mating" devices that farmers use to extract their semen. Introducing some novelty—by changing the location of the device, for example—can reduce the time it takes the bulls to ejaculate.[48] While reducing time to ejaculation is probably not the goal of most human date nights, injecting novelty can inoculate long-term relationships against boredom. And boredom turns out to be a surprisingly potent force that can chip away at even the strongest relationships. Current levels of boredom predict a married couple's overall satisfaction with the relationship almost a *decade* later.[49] Maybe money can't buy love, but it can buy novel, exciting activities. And given the central importance of romantic relationships for human happiness, anything we can do to make time with our partners a treat is money well spent.

The value of novelty extends far beyond romantic relationships, all the way to toilet paper. Toilet paper comes in different colors and textures—Quilted? Did someone's grandmother knit it for you?—but for the most part, it's as commoditized as a product can be. Charmin, however, had a different idea about toilet paper. The company found a way to make using their product a "treat" by providing consumers with something novel and unexpected. How? Take a moment to guess. And keep it clean, please.

If you guessed what they tried, you are a marketing genius. Charmin introduced Potty Palooza, a traveling luxury port-a-potty "adorned with all the amenities you would find at home—from wallpaper and skylights to hardwood floors and televisions."[50] Imagine being at a crowded sports event, expecting the typically horrific bathrooms, and stumbling instead into a toilet paradise. Potty Palooza effectively transforms the mundane act of waste management into a treat.

Adding a dose of novelty can also short-circuit our tendency to consume something that no longer provides pleasure. People in the habit of buying popcorn at the cinema will eat just as much of it whether it is stale or fresh, even though they report getting little enjoyment from the stale stuff.[51] Popcorn lovers might assume that breaking this habit would be tough. But novelty is all it takes. Try this for yourself: Next time you go to the cinema, eat your popcorn with your nondominant hand (if you're a righty, eat with your left hand; if you're a lefty, you probably think you are too unique and creative to be bothered with our tasks). When popcorn lovers eat with their nondominant hand, they free themselves from mindless consumption. They still eat plenty of this salty, buttery treat when it's fresh and delicious, but they leave it aside when it's stale and unsatisfying—when it's no longer a treat.

Can Everyman Become a Silverman?

Practicing Silverman's Mantra demands recognizing how different we are from thermometers. Because the cheerometer is sensitive to both the past and the future, giving something up for a few months or a few minutes can allow us to recalibrate. Just knowing that we have limited access to something, and that it's not an inextricable part of our identity, may help us appreciate it more. Taking a break from some things, like spouses and toilet paper, is both complicated and messy. These cases call for an injection of novelty. Applying Silverman's Mantra is important when—like a skunked Liz at a party—we find ourselves no longer noticing what we've got. These strategies are especially valuable when it comes to treats that cost a little more, where we pay a premium for pleasure: things like lattes, fast cars, and Belgian chocolate bars.

Silverman's Mantra stands in opposition to the ethos of modern America. Whereas American culture values abundance and big purchases (big cars, big homes, big-box shops), French culture emphasizes the value of little treats—*petits plaisirs*.[52] This cultural difference is particularly stark at the dinner table. The French eat less than Americans, taking more time to savor the taste and texture of their food.[53] Even at McDonald's. In a 2003 study, researchers compared a McDonald's in the middle of Paris to a McDonald's in the middle of Philadelphia.[54] Even though a large order of fries was about 30 percent smaller in Paris, Parisians took about 50 percent longer to sit and eat their food than their American counterparts.

In cultures where the Protestant work ethic has taken hold, treats often seem improper, or even immoral—leading people to feel that they should only indulge when they have a good reason for doing so.[55] American university students expect to feel guilty when they splurge on a treat like a spa treatment or dinner out for no particular reason. For most of them, though, these expected feelings of guilt never materialize, overshadowed instead by the pleasure of the treat. Yet they continue to believe they will feel guilty about future indulgences.[56] The little treats of daily life may provide a purer source of pleasure than people realize.

This failure to appreciate the value of treats may push people away from enjoyable experiences. In one study, researchers paid people $2, telling them they could keep the money or use it to purchase a ticket for a lottery.[57] When the lottery prize was a $200 dinner to a gourmet restaurant, 84 percent of people bought a ticket. When the prize was $200 cash, only 65 percent of people bought the ticket. This difference is remarkable. After all, you could use the $200 in cash to buy a $200 dinner, or *anything else* you desired. But the opportunity for a treat in the form of a gourmet dinner provided a more compelling incentive than cash, which most people thought they'd use for boring necessities, such as groceries. Until, that is, the researchers presented the two options side by side. When people had the *choice* between the dinner or the cash, more than twice as many people chose the cash over the dinner. Choosing cash is economically rational, sensible, and defensible—but, given the value of treats, probably detrimental for happiness.

What would you enjoy more, a small, heart-shaped chocolate

(worth fifty cents) or a slightly larger chocolate (worth $2) in the shape of a cockroach? Faced with this choice, most people say they would *enjoy* eating the heart-shaped chocolate more. And yet most people say they would *choose* the cockroach-shaped chocolate.[58] The hard, economic attributes (price, size) win out over the "softer" features (roachiness) during decision-making, even though the softer features matter for enjoyment. This makes sense when choosing vacuum cleaners and other utilitarian products. But when it comes to chocolate and other treats, people may weigh economic considerations to an extent that few economists would condone.[59]

In the heart of Beverly Hills, at the luxurious Four Seasons spa, a ninety-minute massage costs $230, whereas three thirty-minute massages cost a whopping $330. All else being equal, most people report they would rather have a larger number of smaller pleasures, rather than a smaller number of larger pleasures.[60] For example, people prefer to get $5 a day for five days, rather than $25 all on one day. But all else is rarely equal. From an economic perspective, the ninety-minute massage at the Four Seasons is clearly the better deal. But consider whether it's a better deal from *your* perspective. Three thirty-minute massages give you three treats instead of one experience that you'll likely tire of before it's over, providing you with a bigger happiness payoff for each dollar spent.

3

Buy Time

Kathleen and Dennis Morrison have two cats, two hamsters, and two children under the age of three. (Names have been changed to protect the innocent.) While any household with that combination of residents is bound to be a bit untidy, Kathleen's sister Francesca doesn't mince words. "They're slobs," she says. Dennis works long hours at a law firm, and Kathleen, a teacher, detests cleaning. Francesca recalls, "I used to do Kathleen's chores when we were little. Not even little—in high school! We weren't allowed to do fun stuff until we both finished our chores, and cleaning the bathroom took Kathleen all day." Today, a small army of Roombas fills the Morrison household. The robotic vacuum cleaners patrol the floors of their home, picking up pet fur, cookie crumbs, and the other detritus of family life. The newest addition to their fleet is the Scooba, which washes, scrubs, and squeegees their floors. The robots operate on timers, launching into cleaning routines without their masters asking—offering a long-overdue glimmer of the utopian future envisaged on *The Jetsons.* With a price tag over $300, a Roomba costs more than your run-of-the-mill vacuum cleaner. But a Roomba offers something that even high-end traditional vacuums do not: the opportunity to change the way you use your time.

Time and money are frequently interchangeable. Instead of spending four hours reading *People* magazine at the Dallas airport, you could spend an extra $100 for the direct flight from LAX to JFK. But people often sacrifice their time to save small amounts of money, a human foible captured best by a headline in our favorite fake newspaper, the *Onion:*

> ANAHEIM, CA—Thirty-one-year-old Edward Brawley's plan to get himself an umbrella from a random lost and found took two hours, but it saved him $2.99.[1]

Whether driving for an hour to get petrol that is five pence cheaper, waiting in endless lines to get a free food sample, or taking an entire afternoon to abscond with a cheap umbrella, we too often sacrifice our free time just to save a little money.

Many of us wish we had more free time to do more of what we love—for Liz, it's working out; for Mike, playing guitar. In theory, it's possible to use money to buy more of this kind of time. But research suggests that people with more money do not spend their time in more enjoyable ways on a day-to-day basis.[2] Wealthier individuals tend to spend more of their time on activities associated with relatively high levels of tension and stress, such as shopping, working, and commuting.

Since the 1960s, when *The Jetsons* first appeared, average incomes in many countries have risen dramatically.[3] While it's mildly disappointing that we're still without flying cars and sassy robot maids, it is more surprising that rising incomes have not led us to use our time in happier ways over the past four decades.[4] Researchers refer to the amount of time that people spend in an unpleasant mood—when their feelings of tension, depression, or irritation outweigh their feelings of happiness—as the U-index. People are rarely in an unpleasant mood while exercising, praying, reading, or having sex (unless maybe they are trying all these activities at the same time). But unpleasant moods are common while working, commuting, shopping, or doing housework. Over the past forty years, the specific activities people engage in have changed considerably, yet the overall U-index has barely budged. An important and underutilized route to increasing happiness lies in using money to improve our personal U-index.

Buying time isn't always easy, and the strategies below are designed to overcome barriers to applying this principle. Taking this principle seriously means rethinking many everyday expenditures and transforms decisions about money into decisions about time—a kind of mental backflip that can make people more inclined toward happy choices. For companies, putting this idea into practice entails reshaping policies and products, enabling their employees and customers to reap more happiness from the minutes and hours that form the fabric of daily life.

The Illusion of Busyness

At Intel, a typical information technology employee receives 350 emails per week and devotes twenty hours to managing this river of messages. A full 30 percent of these emails are viewed as unnecessary.[5] Intel recently experimented with "email-free Tuesdays," encouraging a group of employees to spend four hours unplugged from email and phones, giving them an uninterrupted period to, you know, *think*.[6] Research shows that employees who feel less harried are happier during their workday.[7] This feeling of time affluence has important implications for happiness once those employees leave work for the day.[8] In one study, more than eight hundred managers and professionals in Turkey reported whether they agreed with statements such as "There have not been enough minutes in the day" and "My life has been too rushed."[9] Workers who agreed with these statements—scoring low in time affluence—were less satisfied with their jobs specifically, but also with their lives overall. They even reported more headaches and sleep problems. Research in the United States suggests that increased time affluence is linked to greater happiness even for people who say that they prefer to be busy.[10]

People who feel pressed for time have difficulty staying in the moment.[11] At the end of yoga class, while the other enlightened attendees sink into a deep state of spiritual relaxation, lying spread-eagled on their mats, Liz can't help but think of the thirty-one things she needs to do right after class. Rather than letting our minds wander to dinner plans or unanswered emails, staying focused on the present moment is beneficial for happiness. In fact, regardless of whether an activity is pleasant or unpleasant, people are happiest when they stay focused on it.[12]

People who feel they have plenty of free time are more likely to exercise, do volunteer work, and participate in other activities that are linked to increased happiness.[13] Although money can be used to buy "free time," in part by outsourcing the demands of daily life such as cooking, cleaning, and even grocery shopping, wealthier individuals report elevated levels of time pressure. In countries ranging from Germany to Korea, people who make more money say they feel more rushed. This holds true even after taking into account the number of hours that they work each week, both inside and outside the home.[14] Around the world, wealthier individuals are more likely to say they felt stressed on the previous day.[15] Greater material affluence may fail to yield more happiness in part because of the diminished time affluence it often brings.

The Slow Movement promises to help people "downshift" to a more relaxed pace of life (for an introduction to everything from slow food to slow books, visit http://www.slowmovement.com). The movement's underlying premise is that we work more and have less free time than in the past. There's just one problem with this assumption: the best research doesn't support it. If anything, the opposite is true. People do say they *feel* busier.[16] And when people calculate how many hours they spend working, they arrive at higher estimates than their counterparts in earlier decades.[17] But this kind of calculation isn't easy. Take thirty seconds to figure out how many hours you worked last week. Did you remember to subtract the time you took off for your dentist appointment, or time spent planning your holiday and gossiping with your coworkers during the workday?

To get around the inaccuracy of self-reports, researchers asked participants to record everything they did for all 1,440 minutes of the day. Comparing recent time diaries to similar diaries from earlier decades revealed that people in the United States spend about four hours more per week engaging in leisure than they did in the 1960s, while work hours have remained relatively constant.[18] Shifting demographics, such as women entering the workforce, can complicate such cross-decade comparisons. But our sense that we have less free time now than people did in earlier decades may be largely an illusion.

A more likely culprit behind the perceived time famine in modern life is financial prosperity. While wealthier people report feeling more pressed for time, simply *feeling* like your time is valuable can make it seem scarce. In a study at the University of Toronto, students played the role of consultants, performing tasks for various offices of a fictitious company and billing their time in six-minute intervals.[19] Half the students billed the company 15 cents per minute ($9/hour) for their time, while the others billed the company $1.50/minute ($90/hour). Afterward, students who billed the company at the higher rate reported feeling more pressed for time—even though they had completed the same tasks for the same amount of time as students who billed at the lower rate. In other words, making students' time worth a lot of money was all it took to turn them into stressed-out, time-squeezed consultants.

Why might this be? From diamonds to Double Downs to women at Star Trek conventions, scarcity increases value. And conversely, when something is valuable, it is typically perceived to be scarce. As time becomes worth more money, people see that time as increasingly scarce.[20] This powerful association may help explain why Americans report feeling more pressed for time than in earlier decades. Rising incomes over the past decades have made time relatively more valuable. The same pattern holds within any one individual's lifetime. Until retirement, most people get wealthier as they age, potentially helping to account for why our lives feel busier than when we were younger.

Is a Minute Saved a Minute Gained?

Given the importance of time affluence, the many time-saving products available today appear to hold substantial promise for increasing happiness. The Roombas largely eliminate what would otherwise be one of the worst parts of Kathleen

Morrison's day, freeing her to spend more time with her children.Although vacuuming seems like a fairly trivial hassle, research suggests that daily hassles exert a remarkable downward force on our happiness. One study of a hundred adults in the San Francisco Bay area showed that psychological distress over a nine-month period was predicted less by major life events than by day-to-day hassles, ranging from "sexual problems" to "troublesome neighbors" to "filling out forms" (three hassles that we hope were unrelated).[21]

We're not suggesting that everyone go out and buy a Roomba as a pathway to lifetime happiness. Some people actually *enjoy* vacuuming. As a single parent, Dan Brand found comfort in the hours he spent vacuuming his home in Concord, Massachusetts. "There were always so many kids and chaos when I was raising four teenagers," he says, "that energetic vacuuming was a way of exerting a certain amount of control, if only for a little while." Dan's unusual enthusiasm for vacuuming underscores the danger of time-saving products. Their widespread availability may spur us to buy things, from two-in-one shampoo to the McSalad Shaker, that are designed to shave minutes off activities we might otherwise *enjoy*, like taking hot showers and eating fresh food (and for Dan, vacuuming). The McSalad Shaker, which can be eaten with one hand on the wheel, allows drivers to get their veggies on the go. When McDonald's first introduced this product, the company's spokeswoman Joanne Jacobs explained, "We do not, not, not advocate eating it while driving." But, she added, "It does fit in a cupholder."[22]

Although products like the McSalad Shaker are carefully engineered to make our daily activities more efficient, potentially enhancing time affluence, new research shows that these products can have ironic side effects. Just seeing fast-food logos makes people more impatient.[23] And when people think about the last time they ate at a fast-food restaurant, they report an increased desire for other time-saving products. Thus products designed primarily to make our daily activities more efficient may actually *reduce* time affluence by intensifying our feelings of impatience, reinforcing our desire for more time-saving products.

Purchases that reduce or eliminate the worst minutes of our day can provide a big happiness bang for our buck, but time-saving products that only increase our efficiency may backfire. If products designed to save us time make us feel as though we have less of it, could the reverse also be true? Could activities that take up time in our busy schedules make us feel as though we have more time available? Because time's high value makes it feel scarce, giving this precious resource away for free can increase feelings of time affluence. When people engage in volunteer work, even for as little as fifteen minutes, they feel that they have more free time in their lives. Near the end of an hour-long study at the University of Pennsylvania, students learned that their final task would involve spending fifteen minutes helping an at-risk student from a local state secondary school by editing his or her university application essay.[24] Half of the students received an essay and a red pen for editing, but the rest were told that all of the essays had been edited and they could leave early. In other words, some students had to stay an additional fifteen minutes to do volunteer work, while others received a "windfall" of free time. The students who stayed to help out reported feeling like they had more free time available compared to students who actually got extra free time by leaving early. Taking the time to help others makes people feel effective ("If I have time to help you, I must be good at getting my own stuff done!"), and these feelings of competence lead volunteers to feel less overwhelmed by the multitude of tasks in their everyday lives. The same fifteen minutes can make us feel either time rich or time poor, depending on how we spend them.

Companies can potentially increase their employees' feelings of time affluence by providing them with opportunities to help others. Since the 1990s, Home Depot has fostered a close relationship with Habitat for Humanity. Employees contribute their expertise to assist with home construction for low-income families.[25] In 2011, Home Depot employees in Canada donated thousands of hours and helped build 244 homes. Paulette Minard, the company's community affairs manager in Canada, explains: "We let our associates in their own community tell us, 'This is the project that's most meaningful in my local neighborhood, where I want to get out and help.'" In the wintry plains of Saskatchewan, employees of Home Depot's Regina store decided to take on a building project and, as Paulette explains, "they went out once a month—every month—in rain and snow" until they completed the home. Regina is known for its extreme weather, and winter temperatures regularly drop below zero in winter. But the pictures of the Regina team show them proudly standing by their construction site, never mind the snow. While Home Depot provides financial support for the building materials, many employees contribute their own time on weekends and holidays. By "giving up" their free time, however, research suggests, these employees may feel *more* time affluent, enhancing their satisfaction with their work and their lives.

Constraining Time

Just as giving time away can make us feel as though we have more of it, other simple changes offer similar unexpected benefits for happiness. Ever bought a family pet? Any new pet comes with new responsibilities, most of which children abdicate within the first week. Given the amount of time owners spend caring for pets, which pets are best? The pet that requires the least amount of our time might be best, leaving us time for exercise and friends. A goldfish, for example, requires just a few minutes to feed each day and the occasional tank cleaning. From this perspective, buying a dog would be a disastrous decision, given the canine's pesky need for attention. And owning a dog costs an average of £1183 a year, making the goldfish look like a steal.[26]

Rather than maximizing free time by avoiding any form of commitment, consider instead how today's purchase will alter how you spend your time tomorrow. A dog, in this view, is actually a catalyst for us to exercise more through walking and games of fetch. Older adults walk more regularly when their walking partner is a dog rather than a friend or spouse.[27] Exercise produces both immediate and long-term benefits for happiness. In general, the more you exercise, the happier you get, at least within reasonable ranges of exertion.[28] But when it comes time to lace up the trainers, people tend to underestimate how much they'll enjoy exercise.[29] Going for a fifteen-minute walk outdoors makes people feel happier and more relaxed than getting similar exercise indoors, but people often fail to appreciate the added value of going outside.[30] That's when the sad puppy-dog eyes looking up at you come in handy. By buying a dog, you're in some sense committing yourself to spend at least fifteen minutes a day walking outside. And you don't have to think hard to realize there are other positive consequences on how you spend your time. Because dogs like to interact with other dogs by sniffing various unmentionable body parts, you get the added happiness boost that comes from chatting with strangers when you meet other dog owners while you're out exercising.

Time in Common

Despite our many idiosyncrasies, humans have a remarkable amount in common, as any happiness researcher from outer space would notice. Although the French may prefer a single espresso while Americans crave a Venti-sized mocha Frappuccino, women in these two countries derive remarkably similar levels of pleasure from common daily activities.[31] And while the Buy Time principle can be applied idiosyncratically, most people would benefit from using their money to change the amount of time they spend on three key activities: commuting, watching television, and hanging out with friends and family.

Commuting

According to the U.S. Census Bureau, Americans spend more than two weeks of the year commuting—more than their typical annual leave.[32] Transportation experts have suggested that developed countries are hitting "peak car," rubbing up against the maximum amount of time that human beings are willing to spend traveling on a daily basis.[33] In both the United States and France, women report being in an unpleasant mood more than 25 percent of the time while commuting, placing this task among the worst-ranking activities in terms of its U-index.[34] And even in Germany, home of the speed-limit-free autobahns, individuals who spend more time commuting report lower life satisfaction.[35] Taking a job that requires an hour-long commute each way has a negative effect on happiness similar in magnitude to not having a job at all. Although accepting a longer commute can provide access to both nicer houses and better jobs, people with longer commutes are no more satisfied with their homes, and they are less satisfied with their jobs. And individuals with long commutes are much less satisfied with their spare time. Commuting, it seems, undermines time affluence.

Most people consider the well-being of their families—not just their own—in deciding whether to take a job. Accepting a longer commute might make for a happier family. But there's no evidence that this is the case. If anything, people report somewhat lower happiness when their spouse has a longer commute.[36] A few years ago, thirty-three-year-old David Mogolov took a copywriting job that required a twenty-five-minute commute, which ballooned to forty minutes in traffic. David recalls the time he spent "sitting in standstill or crawling traffic, listening to honking horns and construction, and witnessing people at their meanest and most disappointed." His wife, Lisa, explains, "I could instantly tell how the evening commute went by his mood when he got home. If traffic was bad and someone cut him off, he'd bring his road rage right into our living room. He'd do everything but honk at me and our daughter."

The average U.S. household devotes almost 20 percent of income to driving expenses. The percentage climbs as high as 40 percent in low-income households.[37] Faced with a lengthy commute, it's easy to see the appeal of devoting even more money to this activity by buying a luxury car. The *average American worker will work five hundred hours a year—two hours out of every work day—just to pay for their cars.*[38] Unfortunately, however, owning a fabulous car does little to mitigate the pain of commuting. As the BMW drivers showed us, people typically don't experience better moods while driving more expensive cars. Rather than taking a higher-paying job farther from home and using the extra money to buy a nice car, most people would be better off sticking with a job closer to home, even if it pays less. To offset the happiness costs of going from no commute to a twenty-two-minute commute, the average person would need to see their income rise by over a third—and that's just to break even.[39] Rather than bugging the boss for a raise, you could get a similar happiness boost, research shows, by moving closer to work.

When it comes to commuting, as with many things, length isn't all that matters. David Mogolov took a new job with an even longer commute, but the location of the company makes it possible for him to take the train to work, rather than drive. "On the train," David explains, "I don't have to make decisions, or interact with other angry people before we're properly caffeinated. I get where I'm going, I'm not angry, and I don't endanger myself. Or others." In a 2011 study comparing almost three hundred commuters traveling from their homes in northern New Jersey to their jobs in New York City, people felt significantly less stressed and disgruntled after taking the train than after driving.[40] Train travel was less effortful and more predictable than driving. "I'm not sure anyone would describe the commuter rail as a Zen garden, but David does arrive home considerably less stressed," Lisa says.

Television

The average Briton spends the equivalent of two *months* per year watching television.[41] In many countries, people spend almost as much time watching TV as they do working.[42] If our choices reveal what we like best, TV must be pretty much the most super-terrific thing ever. And yet, study after study shows that people experience less pleasure while watching TV than while engaging in more active forms of leisure, including walking the dog.[43] More than any other activity, television appears responsible for the failure of the U-index to budge over the past four decades. Although people today spend less time doing unpleasant activities such as household chores, television has sucked up much of this newly available time while providing little emotional payoff.[44] In a sample of over one hundred thousand people from thirty-two European countries, individuals who watched more than thirty minutes of television per day were less satisfied with their lives than people who watched TV for under half an hour.[45] Watching the occasional TV show may be genuinely enjoyable, but devoting two months of the year to the tube is too much.*

Although consumers bought up televisions faster than any other innovation of the twentieth century, including telephones and even refrigerators (a little botulism never hurt anyone, apparently), spending money on TV appears counterproductive for happiness. Products like premium cable and beautiful flat-screen TVs are particularly pernicious because they turn up the volume on TV's siren song, seducing us into devoting more and more time to the tube. It can be remarkably difficult to consider the activities that will be displaced by the acquisition of something new. When we are in the process of

* This complexity underscores an important nuance of buying time. An activity that we enjoy doing for a little while may cease to provide as much pleasure if we spend too much time doing it (what economists call diminishing marginal utility). The best use of money, then, doesn't necessarily lie in *maxing out* the amount of time we spend doing a particular activity, but rather in *optimizing* our use of time across activities.

buying a new TV, we envision having friends over to watch the big game, or enjoying movies with the family. But we fail to consider what purchasing a TV *actually* does to our time. What we are buying is an implicit commitment to plunking ourselves in front of it—often alone—for one-sixth of the next year. If you thought of the purchase in these terms, would you think differently about this investment? What if you were buying one for your children?

To be fair, watching TV has one big advantage: it's cheap. Replacing some of the time you spend watching TV with other, more engaging activities (like going out for dinner with friends or taking an art class) will cost you money. But it is money well spent.

Socializing

If you awaken happiness researchers in the middle of the night and ask them to tell you (quick!) what matters most for human well-being, you'll get the same response: get the hell out of my house. After they calm down, though, we're pretty sure they'll agree on the answer: social relationships. People experience the most positive moods of the day while spending time with family and friends.[46] In the past decade, the emotional benefits of parenthood have been much maligned, with media outlets from *New York* magazine to *Slate* featuring headlines such as Why Parents Hate Parenting and Parents are Junkies.[47] Yet a recent study with a nationally representative sample of Americans revealed that playing with children produced more positive feelings than almost any other common daily activity.[48]

It's often said that the best things in life are free. At first glance, research on the emotional benefits of socializing provides support for this comforting mantra. We don't pay for healthy social relationships by the hour, and we've all heard that money can't buy you love. But can't it? Take a moment to think about how much money you've spent on socializing over the past six months, from date nights to birthday parties. The costs of flights and road trips to visit friends and family add up fast. Even joining coworkers for beers after a long day costs more than opening a six-pack alone on the couch. Similarly the average cost of raising a child to the age of twenty-one in the UK is £222,458.[49]

There's a final time trap that buying stuff springs on us. Our purchases can undermine the amount of time we have available to spend with friends and family, by compelling us to work more to afford the purchases we make to try to improve our family life. In a 2003 poll, over 80 percent of Americans—with and without children—reported wishing they had more time to spend with their families.[50] A substantial minority said they would be willing to accept a pay cut to have more time with family. But many respondents indicated that they couldn't afford to do so, often citing the high costs of housing as the barrier. Yet, as we saw earlier, people who spend more money on housing reap few benefits in terms of happiness. Working long hours to earn more money to provide your children with fancier homes and shinier toys may represent a bad happiness trade-off—especially when doing so comes at the cost of actually spending time playing with them.

Paying Employees Not to Do Their Jobs

Aside from commuting, working is the only activity that produces unpleasant moods more than 25 percent of the time among both French and American women.[51] And in countries as diverse as South Korea and Germany, individuals who work more hours report lower time affluence.[52] Of course, as two people with incredibly fun jobs, we would be the first to acknowledge that work can potentially provide an important source of satisfaction.

At Google, employees are paid not to do their jobs. Shannon Deegan, director of people operations at Google, explains, "We say to our engineers in particular, you can decide to work on anything you think is really cool, outside of your day-to-day job."[53] The freedom to spend up to 20 percent of their time on pet projects provided the impetus for innovations such as Google Sky. A group of engineers with a passion for astronomy wondered what would happen if they turned Google Earth's cameras skyward. "They came up with this phenomenal product where you hold up your phone to the sky and it tells you what stars you're looking at," Deegan recounted. This 20 percent time policy has also led to the development of more down-to-earth products, including Gmail, now one of Google's best-known products. According to some estimates, 50 percent of all new products at Google stem from projects developed on 20 percent time.[54] Although not everyone who's eligible picks up a 20 percent time project, the policy shapes the way Googlers view their work. "When people at Google talk about what they like, it's one of the things they talk about. It's culturally important. Knowing that it exists causes people to feel more free," says Laszlo Bock, senior vice president of People Operations.

Long before *googling* became part of the average kindergartner's vocabulary, employers searched for creative ways to change how workers use their time. As the president of Harvard, Charles Eliot created the first sabbatical program in

1880, providing professors with one-year leaves of absence at half pay.[55] They could study, rest, travel, or do whatever else they desired. Whether the impetus for this program came from Eliot's commitment to improving the quality of life at Harvard or from his desire to poach a famous philologist from another university remains a matter of debate. These twin motives for sabbatical programs—making current employees happier and attracting new ones—underlie their growing adoption in the modern corporate world. At Intel, employees can take an eight-week sabbatical every seven years. In a given year, one out of every twenty employees goes on sabbatical.[56] During sabbaticals, some Intel employees travel or spend time with their families, but many others volunteer or pursue personal passions. One die-hard baseball fan spent his sabbatical on the road, attending baseball games all over the United States. And Intel is serious about it. Employees on sabbatical are cut off from their corporate email accounts, and are banned from checking in with the office.

The program also encourages Intel's workers to resist the blandishments of other firms. *Fortune* magazine considers sabbatical programs when ranking the best companies to work for each year, motivating other companies to explore sabbatical programs of their own. At Patagonia, employees can take fully paid, two-month sabbaticals to work on environmental causes. Lisa Myers, a Patagonia employee, spent her sabbatical tracking wolves in Yellowstone National Park.[57] There's even a company, called YourSabbatical.com, devoted to helping employees figure out how best to spend this windfall of time.[58] Elizabeth Pagano and her mother, Barbara, said the idea for their business came out of their own sabbatical. They left their regular lives behind and set sail on a six-month trip through some of the world's deepest waters. As co-captains, Elizabeth and Barbara learned about themselves and each other, and returned to shore some two thousand miles later with a fresh perspective that still guides how they spend their time each day.

The Swimming Pool Paradox

Buying time sounds easy. But it isn't. Part of the problem stems from an important difference between time and money. If you're tight on money this week, you're likely to assume that you'll be similarly constrained a couple of weeks or months from now. Time constraints, however, feel relatively temporary. Sure, this Tuesday you're too busy to vacuum the house because you've got a dentist appointment, and fifty new emails, and a deadline coming up at work, and a birthday present to buy, and the big game to watch on TV. By contrast, the Tuesdays of the future look remarkably open, with only the occasional activity marked on the calendar. Because the future looks free, we're less inclined to use our money to buy time. But the funny thing about Tuesdays (and the other days of the week) is that they tend to fill up as they get closer.

As a result, many of us have experienced what Gal Zauberman at the University of Pennsylvania terms the "Yes . . . Damn!" effect. We agree to do something far in advance, only to regret it when the time rolls around.[59] In a recent ten-day span, Mike went from Boston to Vegas to Boston to Miami to Boston to Cape Cod to Boston to New York to Boston to Australia. What seemed three months earlier like a fun swing around the world became what can only be described as a travel shitshow. As he scrambled between flights, Mike wondered why he ever thought he had time for all of these trips.

Even when we try to make spending decisions with our future time in mind, it's easy to get tempted by products that have no impact on how we spend our time. Many shop displays maximize customers' ability to perceive subtle differences between products. At mattress shops, customers are encouraged to hop from one bed to the next, allowing them to see how a 500-coil mattress differs from the more luxurious 600-coil model. By testing one mattress after the other, it's easier to appreciate the added comfort of those extra 100 coils. The higher price tag appears reasonable. But for most of us, particularly those in committed relationships, intensive mattress-hopping will end as soon as we leave the shop, making that 100-coil advantage difficult to detect in the future. Research suggests that such quantitative differences between products seem much more important when we compare products side by side than when we're considering one product in isolation.[60] So, while comparison shopping sounds like a smart strategy, this approach can magnify minor differences between products, tempting us to pay more for features that will have no bearing on how we spend our future time.

We don't mean to suggest that the quality of a product never matters. Before getting a real job, Liz bought a $50 used mattress from a random guy's garage. At home with its off-putting smell and broken coils, Liz spent hours struggling to sleep while curled into an awkward position to accommodate the lopsided mattress. When a product falls below a certain basic threshold of quality, it's likely to affect how we use our time. (Picture Liz watching 3 A.M. *Seinfeld* reruns and eating Wotsits rather than trying to sleep on her poor excuse for a mattress.) But the experience of comparison shopping tends to focus our attention on differences between products that lie above that threshold. Faced with a decision between multiple products that differ in their features and price tags, ask yourself whether the differences in features will alter how you spend your time. If the answer is no, go cheap.

Of course, it's not always easy to foresee the many ways that a purchase will affect our time. After acquiring basic items such as a TV and a car, Americans see a swimming pool as the next step in achieving "the good life."[61] Research suggests that people tend to focus on core, central features when contemplating future purchases such as swimming pools.[62] Would-be pool owners imagine enjoying poolside cocktails with friends after work or splashing around with happy children on lazy Sundays. But when making a decision to buy a home in the burbs with that Olympic-size swimming pool, you might also want to think about the hours you'll spend stuck in a car getting from work to your suburban oasis, rather than lounging poolside. And having bought a home with a pool, you have also just bought yourself a lifetime of fishing leaves from a tank of water you built to enjoy your "downtime." Now, some pool owners may argue, "Well, yes, but I just hire a pool cleaning company to clean my pool." And people certainly do use their excess money to such ends. Still, paying someone to clean a pool you won't use because you are stuck in traffic should sound mildly troubling. Many companies do a tidy business removing pools that owners once lovingly installed.

Because the lens of imagination focuses on the foreground of pool ownership (poolside parties! lazy Sundays!) while blurring the background details (clogged filters, long commutes), we suggest a simple exercise before making a major purchase:

Think about Tuesday. Take the time to consider what you'll be doing from morning to night this coming Tuesday. How will the purchase affect you on Tuesday? This simple exercise—thinking about time use on a specific day—helps us make less biased predictions about how much any one thing will influence our happiness.[63]

The Hidden Benefits of Thinking in Terms of Time

Transforming decisions about money into decisions about time has a surprising benefit. Thinking about time—rather than money—spurs people to engage in activities that promote well-being, like socializing and volunteering. In a 2010 study, more than three hundred adults completed a simple task designed to activate the concept of either time or money.[64] One group unscrambled sentences related to time, such as "sheets the change clock" (possible answers: "change the sheets" or "change the clock"). Another group unscrambled sentences related to money ("sheets the change price"). Afterward, everyone decided how to spend the next twenty-four hours. Individuals who unscrambled sentences related to time were more inclined to socialize and engage in "intimate relations" and were less inclined to work. Those who unscrambled sentences related to money showed just the opposite pattern, reporting enhanced intentions to work and diminished intentions to socialize or have intimate relations.

Why? Time and money promote different mind-sets.[65] We view our choices about how to spend time as being deeply connected to our sense of self. In contrast, choices about money often lead us to think in a relatively cold, rational manner.

Focusing on time frees people to prioritize happiness and social relationships.[66] Even a simple sentence-unscrambling task is enough to induce these different frames of mind.

These competing mind-sets can lead people to behave differently within the very same setting. In a study conducted near the University of Pennsylvania, researchers approached people on their way into a café and asked them to unscramble sentences related to time or money, priming one of these two concepts.[67] Then the researchers observed what participants did while they were in the café. Participants who had been primed with money spent more time working while they were at the café, compared to those primed with time. In contrast, participants who had been primed with time devoted more of their stay at the café to interacting with others. As a result of this increased socializing, people who thought about time felt happier by the end of their café visit compared to those who thought about money.

Potential donors contribute more time and more money to charity when they're first asked about their willingness to donate time.[68] Thinking about time makes people focus on the warm glow of giving to others, propelling them to help out however they can. It also increases the appeal of experiential purchases. People waiting in line for an outdoor concert in San Francisco reported how much time or how much money they had spent to see the concert that day.[69] Concertgoers felt more enthusiastic about the event when they thought about the time (versus money) they had spent to be there.

Messages that encourage us to think about time or money are ubiquitous. A content analysis of three hundred ads in magazines ranging from *Cosmopolitan* to *The New Yorker* revealed that almost half incorporated concepts related to either time or money.[70] While ads like these may temporarily influence whether people focus on time or money, we favor a more radical shift. By consistently asking yourself how a purchase will affect your time, your dominant mind-set should shift, pushing you toward happier choices.

Is Time Money?

While we have argued that people should transform decisions about money into decisions about time, traditional wisdom teaches just the opposite. Time is money, after all. And as time becomes more economically valuable—allowing every day to be transformed into more pounds—we are more inclined to view time as money. When Stacey Ashlund, a software engineer, was pregnant with her first child, a family member asked how much maternity leave she planned to take. Stacey replied, "In days or stock value?" Stacey's attitude echoes Benjamin Franklin, who wrote, "Remember that *time* is money. He that can earn 10 shillings a day by his labor, and goes abroad, or sits idle, one half of that day . . . has really spent, or rather thrown away, five shillings."[71] Research shows that embracing Franklin's view of time can undermine happiness. When people see time as money, they find it difficult to reap joy from the unpaid pleasures of daily life.

Try this for yourself.

Step 1: Calculate how many hours you worked in a typical week last year.

Step 2: Total up how many weeks you worked last year and how much you earned before taxes.

Step 3: Calculate your average hourly wage by dividing your annual income by the total number of hours you worked last year.

Done? Now, turn on some music you like and do nothing but enjoy it for about a minute and a half.

If you're like participants in a recent study, you may have had trouble enjoying the music after calculating your hourly wage. When four hundred people listened to a piece of beautiful music, they enjoyed it significantly less if they had followed all three steps above.[72] Calculating our hourly wage pushes us to take Benjamin Franklin's perspective, seeing time as money. And seeing time as money promotes impatience during enjoyable but unpaid activities such as listening to music. Calculating their hourly wage caused people to say that listening to music was a waste of time. They felt impatient for it to end so they could get back to work.

If you earn a salary, calculating your hourly wage may have been a novel experience. But if you're paid by the hour, you're probably aware of how much each hour of your time is worth. Indeed, people paid by the hour are more likely to see time as money.[73] Hourly workers, from entry-level baristas to high-powered lawyers, are more inclined to give up additional time in exchange for additional money.[74] In a national survey of Americans, 32 percent of people paid by the hour reported that they would trade more time for more money, whereas only 17 percent of nonhourly workers found this trade-off appealing.[75] Even if you're no longer paid by the hour, your past experience with hourly payment may still influence you. The effect of being paid by the hour takes about two years to wear off.

As well as propelling people to work more, hourly payment can reduce individuals' willingness to engage in activities that are emotionally, but not financially, rewarding. Hourly workers are less likely to participate in volunteer work. This phenomenon holds true even after taking into account other differences between hourly and nonhourly workers.[76] Thus, seeing time and money as interchangeable resources is wise from an economic perspective, but counterproductive from a happiness perspective.

Rather than seeing time as a vehicle to get more money, we suggest viewing happier time as an end in itself. Mike rejects frequent offers for paid consulting gigs, such that he could (in Liz's words) "sometimes still be mistaken for a homeless guy," part of an effort to keep time free for pursuits that satisfy his nerdy nature—like writing this book. By focusing less on money and more on time, it's easier to use both resources in happier ways.

4

Pay Now, Consume Later

In 1949, after a pleasant evening at a New York City restaurant, Frank McNamara discovered he didn't have any cash.[1] Although his wife swooped in to pay the bill, McNamara soon created the Diners Club card, ensuring that he'd never have to experience that mortification again. Apparently others shared McNamara's desire to avoid such mishaps. Adoption of this proto–credit card soared, soon followed by American Express, MasterCard, and the countless other pieces of plastic that clutter the modern wallet. Solving this immediate problem, however, has had an additional, longer-term effect. The rise of the credit card has not only allowed us to pay without cash, but also allowed us to *pay later*—pushing payment into the indefinite future.

Technological innovations (along with the occasional awkward dinner date) have encouraged us to pay later and consume sooner. The speed with which products purchased from around the globe reach consumers has steadily increased. Services like "same-day delivery" and "next-day shipping" are ubiquitous. Innovations in digital technology have accelerated this trend to what we might call "same-second delivery." In a 2010 poll conducted by the Consumer Electronics Association, peace and happiness ranked at the top of Christmas wish lists. But by 2011, both had been edged out by the iPad.[2] Devices like the iPad allow consumers to download everything from books and games to movies and music in an instant, narrowing the gap between desire and fulfillment to a couple of clicks and a matter of milliseconds. While convenient, this widespread pattern—consuming now and paying later—can be counter-productive for happiness. Instead, you'll get more happiness for your money by following a different principle: *pay now, and consume later.*

A Lesson from Teacher Barbie

One of our students, Deb Baldarelli, learned the benefits of delaying consumption from an unlikely mentor: Teacher Barbie. As a child, Deb asked for Teacher Barbie as a gift, and spent weeks preparing for the doll's arrival. She informed her other dolls that Teacher Barbie would be coming and, to their presumed consternation, helped the dolls prepare to be Teacher Barbie's students. But as all parents know, the allure of new toys is often fleeting. Within days of Teacher Barbie's long-awaited arrival, she was piled in with all the other Barbies, just another doll with D-cups. Nearly all of the pleasure that Deb got from Teacher Barbie came *before* she received the doll. Had the toy arrived right away, Deb would have missed the opportunity to fantasize about just how amazing Teacher Barbie would be, from her bookish chic to her impact on the other toys, helping them learn to read, write, and make something of themselves. The French use the verb *se réjouir* to capture the experience of deriving pleasure in the present from anticipating the future. The *se réjouir* period provides a source of pleasure that comes free with purchase, supplementing the joy of actual consumption.

Our tendency to derive more joy from things coming to us in the future than from things already received extends far beyond plastic toys. In a study of more than one thousand people in the Netherlands, holiday-makers exhibited a bigger happiness boost in the weeks *before* their trip, rather than in the weeks afterward.[3] And people generate even more emotional images of Christmas and New Year's when they imagine these events in November than when they look back in January on their actual experiences.[4] Researchers have suggested that we experience a "wrinkle in time," such that events that lie in the future provoke more emotion than identical events in the past.[5] This wrinkle is worth keeping in mind if you're moving soon. People feel more negative emotion when thinking about helping friends move in the future compared to remembering helping in the past. And they demand nicer thank-you gifts. If you plan to "reward" your friends for helping you move with nothing more than cheap beer and pizza, they're more likely to be satisfied with Foster's and Domino's if you have them over the day after the move rather than the day before.

The looming, emotional power of the future can sometimes be a source of torment. Cancer patients undergoing chemotherapy commonly experience vomiting and other side effects in the twenty-four hours *before* undergoing the treatment.[6] This phenomenon also helps to explain people's curiously negative feelings about Sundays: bloggers use the most positive, happy words[7] and tweets ring out with joy[8] on this day of rest, yet when university students rank their favorite days of the week, they rank Friday (a class day) higher than Sunday (a day off). Why? They spend Sunday haunted by thoughts of Monday. As one student explained, "It's dead, and I think of Monday, which at the time seems terrible to me."[9] In general, however, our minds are more likely to wander to pleasant topics than unpleasant ones in our everyday lives, flitting more to fantasies than fears.[10] So, why do students rank Friday, a day when they have to attend classes, relatively highly? Perhaps because even while stuck in Molecular Biology on Friday at 8 A.M., they can imagine just how amazing their Friday and Saturday nights will be.

The ability to generate pleasant thoughts about the future is a hallmark of psychological health. What separates the suicidal from the rest of us is not an abundance of negative thoughts about the future, but rather an absence of positive ones.[11] When healthy people find themselves in a funk, they tend to generate rosy visions of the future as a means of escaping their current malaise.[12] Anticipating good things produces a distinct pattern of neural activation in the nucleus accumbens, a region of the brain linked to the experience of pleasure and reward.[13] And training ourselves to envision a fantastic future has real benefits. In a 2009 experiment, Belgian adults spent a few minutes every evening for two weeks envisioning several positive events that might happen the next day, from receiving a text message sent by a former flame to eating frites at a café.[14] After two weeks of fantasizing, these mental time travelers exhibited a significant increase in their overall happiness.

Marcia Fiamengo paid Virgin Galactic $200,000 for the privilege of spending six minutes in space, but the value of the trip stems in part from looking forward to it. And Virgin Galactic has done a masterful job of maximizing the pleasure of anticipation for its clients. Not only does Virgin Galactic provide frequent updates, allowing the astronauts to see their dream of space travel edging ever closer, but the company connects the astronauts with each other. Since buying her ticket, Marcia has gotten to know the other astronauts and has even worked with them to raise over a million dollars for science education.[15]

Anticipating experiences that are a little more down-to-earth can also be uplifting. Several innovative companies have introduced product features that make the most of the *se réjouir* phase. Travelers visiting TripAdvisor.com can view pictures and read reviews of hotels, restaurants, and attractions, and sign up for weekly TripWatch emails that provide them with the latest information on their destinations. Although these features have clear value for people making travel decisions by giving them up-to-date information to guide their decision-making, a substantial number of people use TripAdvisor for an interesting additional purpose. Twenty percent of users return to the site *after* booking all the details of their trips, revisiting (and re-revisiting) the pictures of the private beach and the steaming stone spa.[16] From the confines of an office cubicle, that spa probably resembles utopian nirvana. Barbara Messing, chief marketing officer at TripAdvisor, says: "I think of TripAdvisor as being in the happiness business. We are really upstream in the planning process, and I believe that people derive as much pleasure from that phase as from the trip itself. It's the dreaming phase, the fantasizing phase, when they think about how great the tapas and the sangria are going to taste."

Why the Future Is Bright

Why does yet-to-be-consumed sangria taste so sweet? Because the future hasn't happened yet. It's inherently ambiguous, inviting our minds to fill in the details as we would like them to be. People looking toward the future are a little like astronauts peering at the earth from space. And in the words of Ben Gibbard and Jimmy Tamborello of the rock band the Postal Service: "Everything looks perfect from far away." This property of the mind helps explain why the sangria of the future is always filled with our favorite fruits—and why an online dater who has experienced a string of bad dates still expects to have a magical evening with a guy who just "poked" her to express his interest.[17] He describes himself as "a real clown," leading her to assume that he's the life of the party. She fantasizes about the years of laughs they'll share together with their future children, Caitlin and James, only to discern on their first date from his attire and face paint that he meant it literally.

A newly elected leader also allows us to envision a rosy future absent the buzzkill of reality. As one member of Parliament described former prime minister Tony Blair: "Blair's like a very sweet pudding. The first mouthful is nice, but then it becomes nauseating."[18] In the United States, almost every president enters office with higher approval ratings than when he leaves it. By then he has screwed up his reputation by, you know, doing stuff. (One exception to the downward trend is Bill Clinton, due primarily to his low initial ratings, which left him with less room to fall.)[19]

The inherent uncertainty of the future not only allows us to view it in a more positive light, but also keeps our attention focused on it. A product we want but don't yet own is like a distant image coming into focus. It captures our attention because we don't know exactly how it will turn out. In one study, students at the University of Virginia viewed an array of small gifts, from Godiva chocolates to university-branded mugs, and chose the two they liked best.[20] Some students were told which one of their favorite gifts they would receive, while others got the good news that they would receive both gifts. A third group learned something more uncertain. They would receive one of their two favorite gifts in a few minutes, but they weren't told which one. Given the chance to look at pictures of the gifts while they waited, those students who didn't yet know which gift they would receive gazed at the pictures the longest. And by the end of the experiment, they felt even happier with their single gift than students who received *both* gifts.

A company called Birchbox capitalized on the pleasures of uncertainty to transform the market for sample-size cosmetics, those mini-tubes of mascara and baubles of liquid blush often tossed in the bottom of beauty counter shopping bags. Founders Katia Beauchamp and Hayley Barna wanted to make these throwaway products valuable, or as they put it, "delightful."* For $10 a month, Birchbox members receive a small pink box in the mail filled with beauty samples. Hayley explains that when the monthly email notifies members that the boxes have shipped, "Twitter blows up. Everyone starts freaking out that their box is coming."[21] The key? Uncertainty. Early on, the Birchbox team decided they wouldn't let members choose which products to receive—or even inform them ahead of time what each month's box would contain. When that email goes out, everyone tries to figure out what's coming. Members search the web and YouTube, looking for scraps of information about what's in the box. Bloggers develop an instant following

* Full disclosure: Mike advised Hayley and Katia on Birchbox as his students at Harvard Business School. Luckily, there's no conflict of interest. Mike has not received a single free sample of Queen Medieval Tinted Lipstick Treatment for his efforts.

if they have a particularly speedy postal worker who gets the box to them first.

But there is a tension here: People are driven to reduce their uncertainty by finding out what's in the box. Yet successfully accomplishing this goal—taking away the uncertainty—can also take away the fun. The same region of the brain that responds when we anticipate something good (the nucleus accumbens) loses interest once we've gotten it.[22] Birchbox provides members with detailed online information about the products in each box, and the team strives to release this Web content once most people have their boxes. Inevitably, though, some people stumble across it before their box has arrived. And then, Katia explains, "They get livid! They send us nasty messages." In the absence of surprise, the contents of the box feel more like those old samples strewn in the bottom of shopping bags. But with the critical ingredient of uncertainty, Birchbox is, as one member put it, "like Christmas every month."

Uncertainty itself is neither sweet nor sour; rather, it intensifies the flavor that's already there. Birchbox customers know that their boxes will be filled with the latest and greatest from the world of cosmetics. But people also spend money on things that produce a combination of positive and negative emotions, like the Tough Mudder events. Think of it as titillation lined with trepidation. The excitement that comes from looking forward to playing in the mud on event day may be tempered by some anxiety about how much pain the race is going to induce. Because uncertainty can magnify both positive *and* negative emotions, delaying consumption is a safer strategy for purchases that inspire purely positive feelings—purchases that are "delightful" rather than, say, "complicated."

Why Drooling Makes It Taste Better

Part of the reason that we are built to experience such a range of emotional responses, from delight to despair, is to navigate our uncertain futures.[23] If you're deciding whether to join friends on a trip to Hawaii, you can simulate this holiday in your mind in a matter of seconds. The degree of delight you feel provides a clue to guide your decision. Right now, imagine yourself riding a unicorn on the rings of Saturn. The ability to conjure up an image of this awesome and impossible activity contributes to the magic of being human, and demonstrates our ability to go almost anywhere in our minds.

When the mind travels to the future, it often arrives in a place that differs from reality in reliable ways, with the rough edges smoothed out and the pleasing details filled in. But by building anticipation, do we set ourselves up for a fall? Most people can probably think of a past experience intended to be pleasant that turned out differently than expected. Liz went to Oahu several years ago to enjoy surfing the warm, blue waves of the north shore, only to get attacked by a ten-foot tiger shark. Mike tried Diet Coke Lime.

While these dramatic chasms between expectation and reality are memorable, they have been relatively rare in our own lives (online dating experiences notwithstanding). But almost every day, there are relatively minor cracks between what we imagine and what we experience. Luckily, our brains have yet another trick to help us. When these minor mismatches occur, positive expectations can fill in the cracks, enabling us to experience the reality we expected. In one study, people led to believe that a set of cartoons would be funny ended up laughing more.[24] In another, people led to believe a politician would perform well in a political debate viewed his performance more positively than those who had been told he was under the weather.[25]

Because consuming later provides time for positive expectations to develop, delaying consumption also increases our ability to smooth over the cracks. This property holds true even for something as simple as a video game. In a study at the University of Southern California, students got the most pleasure from playing a video game if they first spent a minute imagining how much fun it would be.[26] This waiting period was particularly beneficial for players who knew a few concrete details about the game they would be playing, enabling them to generate positive expectations—much like would-be travelers on TripAdvisor. Creating a *se réjouir* period improved players' experience even when the game was lower in quality than they expected. Poring over pretty pictures and positive reviews on TripAdvisor is likely to enhance our subsequent enjoyment of a Hawaiian holiday, even if the pool's a little smaller than we expected and the sangria's a little less fruity. All bets are off, though, once a tiger shark appears.

Delay can enhance the pleasure of consumption not only by providing an opportunity to develop positive expectations, but also by enhancing what we call the "drool factor." The very best stimulus for studying the drool factor? Chocolate. In a recent experiment, university students chose whether they wanted a Hershey's Kiss or Hershey's Hug.[27] They either ate their chosen chocolate immediately or waited thirty minutes. When students had to wait for their candy, they enjoyed it more and expressed more interest in buying additional Hershey's chocolates. Even though they didn't learn anything new about the chocolates, the delay provided an opportunity to build visceral desire, to drool a bit. Indeed, students who waited for the chocolate reported being more likely to visualize eating it prior to consumption. Similar effects emerged for soda. After picking out their favorite brand, consumers enjoyed drinking it more if they had to wait twenty-four hours rather than sucking it down on the spot. The benefits of delay do not extend to prune juice, however. Unlike with lemons, when life gives you prunes, apparently you cannot make prune-ade out of it.

So, when is delaying consumption most beneficial in getting the biggest happiness bang for your buck?

- When the delay provides an opportunity to seek out enticing details that will promote positive expectations about the consumption experience, as well as excitement in the interim. Think TripAdvisor and Birchbox.
- When anticipating the purchase makes you drool, increasing the pleasure of eventual consumption. Think Hershey's Hugs. In contrast, we do not recommend delaying neutral necessities like oil changes or unenviable expenses like root canals, which produce a more unwelcome form of drool.
- When the consumption experience itself will be fairly fleeting. Think spaceflights. In these cases, delay provides a valuable opportunity to draw out the pleasure beyond the experience itself.

Would You Pay for a Delay?

People will only seek out opportunities to postpone consumption if they recognize the value of delay. But this insight is surprisingly elusive. While students who waited to eat a

Hershey's Kiss enjoyed it more than students who ate it right away, these same individuals failed to recognize the benefits that delay provided. They didn't *think* they'd enjoyed the chocolate any more than usual.[28] Because the wait itself was unpleasant, they stated that they would rather just eat the chocolate right away next time. Worse still, students who only *imagined* eating the chocolate thought that the delay would make them enjoy the Kiss less than if they ate it immediately.

Why do we fail to recognize that consuming later can enhance enjoyment? Research shows that when something nice is available immediately, the "power of now" dwarfs all else. Yes, the future is more compelling than the past, making each day of anticipation more valuable than each day of reminiscence, but there is nothing so evocative as the present. Consider how happy you would be if someone gave you a £25 Starbucks gift card today, or if you received the same surprise on a random day three months from now. Unless your love for Frappuccinos slowly withers with each passing day, you should probably expect to be about as happy regardless of whether you receive the gift card today or in three months. Free coffee is free coffee. But when people contemplate these scenarios, they predict that receiving the gift card would provide more joy now than it would if they received it in three months.[29] Due to the power of now, people overvalue the present, making it difficult to appreciate the potential benefits of delay.*

Even in those cases where people *do* recognize the benefits of a delay, they may be unwilling to pay for the added value

* Another reason we may devalue the Frappuccinos of the future is that we simply don't care as much about our future selves as we do about our present selves. Mike-of-Today may see Mike-of-the-Future almost as a different person. So, he might as well buy himself a Frappuccino today rather than providing one for his wizened future self.

that delay provides. Asked to choose between attending a concert by their favorite band tomorrow or in two weeks, some 60 percent of people recognized that waiting two weeks would confer the added benefit of anticipation, providing them with two weeks of extra happiness.[30] But when asked about their willingness to pay for the two concerts, only 19 percent of people reported that they would pay more to attend the concert in two weeks. When people think about spending money, they follow the seemingly sensible rule that they shouldn't pay for a delay. This rule creates a rare situation in which people are undermined by their own self-discipline. Because conscientious individuals are inclined to follow rules, they show the biggest disconnect, refusing to pay for a delay despite recognizing that the delayed concert would provide more pleasure.

A study that examined another kind of kiss found an apparent exception to our unwillingness to pay for delays. Offered the opportunity to buy a kiss from their favorite movie star, people were willing to pay over 50 percent more to postpone the kiss for three days, presumably to savor seventy-two hours' worth of thoughts about this fabulous but fleeting experience.[31] Because celebrities rarely work as research assistants, though, this choice was hypothetical. Had Ryan Gosling and Scarlett Johansson strolled in and started doling out kisses, we suspect that people's desire to enjoy three days of anticipation would have been overwhelmed by the desire to have the kiss right *now*.

In short, delaying consumption can enhance pleasure, but people don't always recognize the benefits of delay. Even when they do, they may balk at the idea of paying for it. This paradox creates a pickle for companies looking to maximize both their profits and customers' happiness. There is substantial room, then, for innovation in both real and virtual waiting rooms. While Kayak.co.uk searches the Web for your flight from London to Lanzarote, the site gives you a real-time update of the work it's performing (now searching Iberia . . . now searching Aer Lingus . . .). Research shows that waiting can increase satisfaction if customers get the impression that work is being done on their behalf during the delay.[32] This "labor illusion" is so powerful that it leads customers to prefer services that make them wait to services that provide the same quality immediately.

The Pain of Paying Now

The drives to consume now and to pay later are both propelled by the power of now. Because there's no time as evocative as the present, we are motivated to expedite the good (consumption) and postpone the bad (payment). Like *Seinfeld*'s George Costanza, we would be well-advised to recognize our instincts—and then do the opposite. We've seen the benefits of delaying consumption, but what about the other half of the equation: paying now?

The feeling of parting with hard-earned cash can be so aversive that behavioral economists have given it an ache-inducing name: "the pain of paying."[33] This turn of phrase is more than a metaphor. When people think about recent expenditures, they become more susceptible to actual, physical pain.[34] Neuroeconomists have found some evidence that facing high prices can activate regions of the brain associated with anticipating real, stub-your-toe style pain. In a study at Stanford University, participants went "shopping" from the inside of a brain scanner.[35] Desirable products like Godiva chocolates popped up on the computer screen followed by the price of the product, and people decided whether to purchase each product. Viewing enticing products promoted activation in the nucleus accumbens (the brain region linked to positive anticipation). But when a price appeared that participants considered excessive, their brains exhibited activation in the insula, a neural region that responds to diverse forms of impending pain. Activation in both the nucleus accumbens and the insula predicted individuals' decisions about whether to purchase each product. Contemplating the purchase of something as simple as a box of chocolates can trigger a blend of both pleasure and pain, shaping our decisions about whether to reach for our wallets.

Because the pleasure of consumption is purest without the experience of paying for it, *anything* we can do to separate payment from consumption can enhance the pleasure of the purchase. Many people solve this riddle by consuming immediately, and paying later. But while paying later solves one problem, it creates another.

The Lure of Paying Later

Hundreds of years ago, villagers on the western Pacific island of Yap adopted the most concrete form of currency imaginable: giant stone disks that required as many as twenty people to move.[36] These stones, quarried and carved on another remote island, were used to pay for major expenses. All currencies rise and fall. This one sank. According to legend, while crossing the sea with one of the stones, a crew of villagers encountered a terrible storm. In the chaos of the waves, the precious stone was lost. When the crew returned to Yap empty-handed, the villagers decided that the sunken stone still counted as currency. Even though it lay at the *bottom of the sea*—effectively existing only in the villagers' minds—the stone was money. And so, on this remote island, money made the move from concrete entity to abstract concept.

This story echoes our own recent history. In the twentieth century, the United States saw a decline in the use of cold, hard currency. The government dropped the gold standard, and diverse forms of credit became increasingly available. As we all know too well, this shift eventually created some problems. The satirical newspaper the *Onion* captured this zeitgeist when they ran a story in 2011 with the headline "Visa Exposed As Massive Credit Card Scam."[37] According to the mock news article, "Visa posed as a reputable lender, working through banks to peddle a variety of convincing-looking credit cards carefully designed to dupe consumers into spending far more money than they had." R. Neil Williams—ostensibly a former executive at Visa—explained: "Sure, people should have known better than to trust a magical card that allowed them to buy anything they want without any money whatsoever. But at Visa we understood that people will believe anything if they want it bad enough. That was the genius of our whole scheme."

Research suggests that credit cards are an ingenious innovation (or scam, depending on your perspective) for getting people to spend more money. These pieces of plastic provide anesthesia against the immediate pain of paying. When students had the opportunity to bid on a pair of tickets to a sold out sporting event, those told they would have to pay with cash by the next day bid an average of $28 for the tickets. Their peers who used credit cards bid an average of $60.[38] These students were not financially naïve freshers, but rather MBA students who should have known better than to pay a 100 percent premium for the privilege of using credit rather than cash. Because credit cards minimize the pain of paying at the time of purchase, they promote a kind of detachment that makes even smart, savvy individuals more amenable to parting ways with their money. This detachment also makes it harder to remember how much we've spent. When researchers asked thirty people to estimate their credit card expenses before opening their monthly bill, *every single individual* underestimated the size of their bill—by an average of almost 30 percent.[39]

This problem may compound over time. American households had an average of more than $6,000 in credit card debt in 2010.[40] Nearly one-third of credit card users reported carrying a balance rather than paying off their cards at the end of the month.[41] Although taking on debt can be necessary, and sometimes even sensible, credit cards create a potential trap. The power of now makes people believe that paying for something in the future will produce less misery than paying today. If paying is aversive, surely it is wise to put it off for as long as possible. The problem is that just the opposite is true. Almost half of U.S. residents report worrying about their debts.[42] Although the relationship between income and happiness is fairly weak among Americans, there is a much stronger relationship between individuals' happiness and whether they have difficulty paying their bills.[43] In other words, what we owe is a bigger predictor of our happiness than what we make. In Britain, households with more debt exhibit lower happiness.[44] Debt is particularly detrimental for marriage. Married couples with higher levels of debt show increases in marital conflict about everything from sex to in-laws.[45] Paying later may increase the pleasure of consuming now, but the depressing effect of dread can outweigh the buoying effect of pleasure.[46] If you carry a credit card balance that fills you with dread, the happiness boon of paying it off may be greater than just about anything else you could do with your money. The emotional benefits of paying off debt can even dwarf the benefits of building savings[47] (though savings have an important role to play as well).

Making Mojitos Taste Free

All of the research we've described points to a common conclusion: making payments highly salient—whether at the moment of purchase or in the form of accumulated debts—can diminish the pleasure of consumption. If you've ever been in a taxi during a night out on the town, you've probably experienced this problem. The constant ticking of the meter makes it hard to enjoy the ride, as the bill climbs higher with each minute and every mile. And if you happen to be paying a babysitter during the night out, your mental meter may keep ticking even after exiting the taxi, with every additional half hour of date night making a "ka-ching" noise in your head.

Now imagine that you had prepaid for both the taxi and the babysitter the previous week. At the moment you paid, you would still experience the pain of paying. You have to suck it up at some point. But how might prepayment change your evening? The ticks of the taxi meter would be less salient, and the time with your spouse less monetized. During their date nights, Elizabeth Haines and her husband, Terry, solved the child-care problem through a clever "pay now" strategy, relying on the magic of bundling. Because they needed afternoon child care during the week, they hired someone who could take care of the kids during weekday afternoons *and* on date night, bundling it all together into one weekly payment. "I posted the job ad as five afternoons plus one late night, so I never think that I have to pay extra for that night out," Elizabeth explains.

Liz took a related approach to her destination wedding in Mexico, encouraging her guests to spend several days at the all-inclusive resort where the wedding was held. Because the guests paid for their stay months in advance, they could enjoy meals, drinks, and activities without ever reaching for their wallets. At most hours of the day, guests could be found sipping margaritas or mojitos and exclaiming something along the lines of "It's so tasty because it's free!" Of course, the drinks were not free (though some ambitious guests did consume enough to keep their average drink cost remarkably low), but because the all-inclusive holiday had been paid for months earlier, they *tasted* free.*

Katia and Hayley hear similar comments from their clients at Birchbox. As Hayley explains, "People call Birchbox 'free' all the time." Most customers are billed at the beginning of the month and receive their box about two weeks later, effectively separating payment and consumption. And 20 percent of customers pay up front at the beginning of the year, allowing them to enjoy twelve pink boxes with the pain of payment long behind them.

Given the value of paying sooner rather than later, there may be an upside to the recent economic downturn. Consumers are more reluctant to use credit, instead reaching for

---

* Again, no matter when we pay, we have to experience the pain of parting with our money sooner or later. Some of Liz's guests surely experienced an unpleasant twinge back when they paid for the trip. But it seems like a particular shame when the pain of paying coincides with the pleasure of consumption, interfering with our ability to derive happiness from the very thing we're paying to enjoy.

the "pay now" plastic of debit cards. In the second quarter of 2008, as the financial crisis took hold, the retailing giant Target reported that the percentage of purchases paid for by credit card declined for the first time in memory, while the use of debit cards increased.[48] From Middle America[49] to Malaysia,[50] debit card use has surged in recent years. Using this "pay now" plastic reduces spending. A large U.S. study found that debit card users had almost 400 percent less unsecured debt than people who didn't use debit cards, even after taking into account personal characteristics such as income and credit history.[51]

While debit cards make it easier to pay now, potentially reducing debt and increasing happiness, other technological innovations provide tempting new ways to pay later. An app called Card Case, launched in late 2011 (and later rebranded with the name Pay with Square), allows users to link their phones to their credit cards and to pay for purchases without even reaching for their wallets. As soon as a customer approaches a participating merchant, a tab automatically opens in the customer's name. Farhad Manjoo, a user and tech writer, marveled that, "You don't have to pull out your phone, you don't have to open the app, you don't have to sign, swipe, or wait for change. As long as your phone is on your person while you're in the store—in your pocket or in your purse—Card Case can authorize your payment without you having to do a thing."[52] When Farhad used Card Case to buy a cupcake at a San Francisco bakery, "The experience was magical—almost creepily so. It happened so quickly, and lacked so many of the hassles of a normal transaction, that when I left the store with the cupcake it was hard not to feel like I'd just pulled off a heist." We have to admit that this form of payment sounds cool. But the research reviewed in this chapter suggests that innovations such as Card Case may cost us in the long term by promoting the illusion that we can have our cupcake and eat it, too.

From the Grocery Shop to the County Fair

In addition to increasing the pleasure of anticipation and the joy of consumption, paying now and consuming later can make our other spending principles easier to follow. Perhaps you've decided to buy more experiences, and fewer material things. This resolution may waver when you're faced with the immediate, concrete benefits of a new high-end toaster or mattress. But when you won't consume something right away, it's easier to see the more abstract advantages of experiences.[53] Paying now and consuming later can help us take the long view, turning us into better stewards of our own well-being. When people pay for groceries with cash rather than cards, they tend to fill their baskets with peaches, muesli, and other healthy products. They are less likely to leave with armfuls of impulse purchases like cookies and cheesecake.[54] Cash makes paying more painful, and this immediate pain undermines the pleasure of cruising the cookie aisle. Delaying consumption provides a similar benefit. People are more likely to make healthy purchases from an online grocer when there will be a longer delay between order and delivery.[55]

But come on, cookies and cheesecake are delicious! What happened to "Make It a Treat?" Delaying consumption does *not* drive people to unmitigated self-denial. Rather, it drives them to maximize their happiness, whatever form that takes. Indeed, when consumption lies in the relatively distant future, people may be more inclined to follow our advice to take advantage of opportunities for treats. At an airport in the United States, several hundred women received a lottery ticket and a choice between two prizes:[56]

- A luxurious one-hour facial cosmetic treatment or a one-hour pampering massage (maximum retail value = $80) at a premium day spa at the location of your choice
- $85 in cash (you decide how to spend the money—for example, at the supermarket, petrol station, or at a premium day spa at a location of your choice)

When women thought the lottery would take place the next week, only a small minority (18 percent) chose the spa package as their preferred prize. But when they thought the lottery would take place over two months later, twice as many women (36 percent) opted to receive the spa package. Why would anyone choose the $80 spa package over the $85 cash, which could, as the prize description explicitly noted, be used to pay for a trip to the spa? One woman explained why she turned down the cash option: "I would probably spend [it] on something I need rather than something I'd really enjoy! I've been saying for 4–5 months that I'm going to go to the spa for a massage."[57] From a distance, when focused on consuming later, it can be easier to recognize the value of indulging in an occasional treat.

People view the distant future abstractly, prompting them to think about how *desirable* a particular course of action would be. They tend to focus more on *feasibility* when contemplating the immediate future.[58] A busy working mom can appreciate in the abstract how worthwhile it would be for her to take an hour to herself to relax and enjoy a pampering massage. But in thinking about getting a massage today, she may concentrate on the logistical challenges of making it happen. By making purchases that we consume later, it can be easier to choose things that we know are good for our own well-being. And not just healthy vegetables, but also treats like massages.

When it comes time for consumption, having paid long ago brings a final payoff: freedom from the tyranny of sunk costs.[59] Imagine that you bought nonrefundable tickets to opening night at the annual town fair. When the evening rolls around, you have a stomach ache and the thought of candyfloss and amusement park rides makes you feel sick. If you paid for those tickets just that morning, you might decide to go anyway, even though suffering through five hours at the fair won't bring your money back. At first glance, this problem seems like a good argument for delaying payment until the last minute. You don't want to end up feeling forced to do something that's no longer appealing just to justify having paid for it. But paying far in advance solves this problem, too. When payment lies in the distant past, the sunk cost of the tickets doesn't seem like such a looming loss. Purchases that have been paid for long ago feel free, thereby liberating people to spend their time in happier ways, rather than clutching their tummies riding the teacups.*

Paying now and consuming later can help solve the sunk cost problem, but some financially savvy readers may not approve of the advice in this chapter. When Liz presented our spending principles at a conference, attendee Amy Summerville nodded and smiled. But at this principle, her face twisted

* There are some advantages to having paid for things in the recent past, especially for activities we're tempted to skip. We're more likely to go the gym right after having paid our monthly fee, but as that sunk cost recedes into the past, attendance declines. See John T. Gourville and Dilip Soman, "Payment depreciation: The behavioral effects of temporally separating payments from consumption," *Journal of Consumer Research* 25, no. 2 (September 1998): 160–74.

in horror. Growing up, Amy had been drilled by her father, an accountant, on the time value of money. This central tenet of finance is based on the idea that money earns interest over time. Put £100 in an account with a 3 percent interest rate today and in one year, the £100 becomes £103. Amy learned she should delay payment whenever possible, thereby hanging on to her money and earning interest for as long as she could. All else being equal, the maths that Amy learned from her dad makes complete sense, as long as the goal is to maximize your money. But should that be the goal? Single-mindedly pursuing this goal may be overrated. It may be time to consider how to use your money not just to get more *money*, but to get more happiness.

We realize that it is not feasible to delay all consumption into the future. We need to eat *something* today, whether vegetables or cookies. It may be wise to heed the sage advice provided on the label of a candy that explicitly encourages at least some delayed consumption even while indulging the power of now—Now and Laters, which encourage fans to "Eat Some Now. Save Some for Later." What would consumption look like if we lived by the "pay now, consume later" mantra? Take iTunes, the paradigmatic "consume now, pay later" service. Purchases download almost instantaneously, and because users have given Apple their credit card information, notification of payment arrives much later. Consumers would get more happiness bang for their iTunes buck if they forced themselves, after downloading their music, to wait—at least minutes, better hours, and ideally days—before listening. In fact, Mike has gotten into the habit of "preordering" albums on iTunes. The feeling of having purchased the album subsides, and then days or weeks later a "free" album arrives.

It's difficult to overcome the power of now, but it's possible to harness this force. As the pleasures and pains of the present appear particularly intense in the mind's eye, we are most reluctant to make purchases when the pain of paying is immediate and the pleasure of consuming distant. Businesses recognize this psychological phenomenon, which has driven the development of financial and technological innovations that enable people to consume sooner and pay later. By putting this fundamental principle into reverse, you can buy more happiness while spending less money.

5

Invest in Others

Let's begin with two stories about Mike.

Story #1. One day about four years ago, Mike opened his mailbox to find the usual assortment of junk mail and mildly threatening notes from Liz to work on one of our papers. As usual, he tossed both in the trash. On this day, though, there was an unusual piece of mail waiting: a gift certificate from a retailer from whom Mike had bought some silverware, offering Mike the rare chance to be a good person. How? This retailer sent Mike a $50 voucher that he could use—not to buy their products—but to make a donation to a not-for-profit called DonorsChoose.org. Intrigued, Mike went online. DonorsChoose.org is a website that enables state school teachers in the United States, many working in low-income communities, to request items that their students need. Donors can then help those students directly. Do you believe kids aren't being exposed to enough great literature? You can buy copies of *Tom Sawyer* for a fifth-grade class in Lynn, Massachusetts. Fancy yourself an amateur scientist? You can buy a microscope to donate to a classroom of ninth graders in New Orleans. Mike chose a project and donated, felt briefly like the world's best person, and moved on with his life.

Story #2. One day about three years and six months ago, Mike decided he needed a new couch. Having not bought furniture, well, *ever*, Mike went to a retailer he had a good feeling about—Crate & Barrel—where he'd bought some silverware a while back. Mike looked through the options, picked a couch, and then decided that since he was getting a couch, he might as well get a coffee table, too. And why not throw in a matching end table? Thankfully, he (mostly) stopped there.

The second story is a lot more mundane than the first, but they share a critical link: Crate & Barrel. Because Mike has a terrible memory, he had forgotten about his donation experience when he went furniture shopping. Yet he can't help but wonder if his decision to splurge on those extra tables may have had something to do with lingering good feelings toward Crate & Barrel, the retailer that gave him the opportunity to donate. For just a $50 charity voucher, Crate & Barrel won Mike as a customer for life in a way that a $50 gift voucher never could have.

This mixing of charity and commerce between Crate & Barrel and DonorsChoose.org is far from an exception. Even business icon Warren Buffett has recently turned his thoughts to charity, challenging the richest of the rich to pledge at least 50 percent of their wealth to charitable causes. (He's flexible on whether the giving happens during your lifetime or after you pass on.) Buffett himself pledged to give away 99 percent of his wealth. Does Buffett regret his decision to give away his money? Hardly. He claims he "couldn't be happier" with the decision.[1]

Mike and Warren's experiences with charity bring two questions to mind. While Buffett claims his happiness increased when he gave, do the rest of us need to give away billions to get happy from giving? And what happens when charity and commerce mix, when companies engage their customers and employees in acts of charity as opposed to the same old kinds of incentives like vouchers for customers or yearly bonuses for employees? New research shows that spending even small amounts of money on others can make a difference for our own happiness. And we'll see that rewarding customers and employees with opportunities to invest in others—from kids in distant countries to coworkers in the next cubicle—can enhance not only individuals' well-being, but also the company's bottom line.

More broadly, this chapter outlines a principle quite different from the four we have discussed in the previous chapters. Whether encouraging you to buy a trip to the moon or take a break from your daily latte, each of the principles thus far has been geared toward changing how you spend money on *yourself.* Now we'd like you to contemplate an even more radical idea. Rather than think about the different ways you can spend your money on yourself to maximize your own happiness, consider investing it in others. Spending money on others can increase your happiness even more than spending your cash on yourself, but you have to be willing to make yourself a little poorer to reap these benefits.

A Mysterious Envelope

On a fine summer morning in Vancouver, British Columbia, our graduate student Lara Aknin (now a professor at Simon Fraser University) approached passersby with a box of envelopes, and an unusual request: "Would you be willing to be in an experiment?" If people said yes, she asked them how happy they were, got their phone number, and then handed them one of these mysterious envelopes.[2] When people opened the envelope, they found a $5 bill, accompanied by a simple note. For some of them, the note instructed:

> Please spend this $5.00 today before 5pm on a gift for yourself or any of your expenses (e.g., rent, bills, or debt).

Others found a note that read:

> Please spend this $5.00 today before 5pm on a gift for someone else or a donation to charity.

In addition, some people got similar envelopes, but with a $20 bill rather than a $5. Armed with this extra bit of cash and their instructions about how to spend it, people went on their way. That evening, they received a call asking them how happy they were feeling, as well as how they had spent the money. What did people spend the money on? As you can imagine, it varied a great deal by what their slip of paper told them to do. People instructed to spend the money on themselves bought earrings, coffee from Starbucks, and sushi. But what about people told to engage in what we call "prosocial spending," by making a donation to charity or buying a gift for someone else—by giving it away? These individuals reported buying toys for younger relatives, as well as giving money to the homeless. Some of them also bought food or coffee, but with a crucial twist: they bought these treats for someone else.

How did these purchases affect people? By the end of the day, individuals who spent money on others were measurably happier than those who spent money on themselves—even though there were no differences between the two groups at the beginning of the day. And it turns out that the amount of money people found in their envelopes—$5 or $20—had no effect on their happiness at the end of the day. How people spent the money mattered much more than how much of it they got.

This experiment suggests that spending as little as $5 to help someone else can increase your own happiness. You might be wondering: Am I giving enough away right now? Take a moment to fill out the boxes below with the typical amount you spend per month in each of the categories.

Expenses, Rent, Bills, Debt	£
Gifts for Yourself	£
Gifts for Others	£
Donations to Charity	£

Now sum up the first two categories (expenses/bills/rent/debt and gifts for yourself) to calculate your total *personal spending* and sum up the last two (gifts for others and donations to charity) to calculate your total *prosocial spending*. Next, divide your personal spending by your prosocial spending. What's your ratio?

In a representative sample of more than six hundred Americans, personal spending accounted for the lion's share of most people's budgets.[3] The average ratio of personal to prosocial spending was more than 10 to 1. But the amount of money individuals devoted to themselves was unrelated to their overall happiness. What *did* predict happiness? The amount of money they gave away. The more they invested in others, the happier they were. This relationship between prosocial spending and happiness held up even after taking into account individuals' income. Amazingly, the effect of this single spending category was as large as the effect of income in predicting happiness. If you've been focusing on trying to make more money, remember that giving some of it away can be just as rewarding as getting more of it.

Once again, we've seen that Buffett offers the best investment advice. In this case, though, his advice to invest in others pays off in the form of happiness, rather than cash. Of course, Buffett was the first to acknowledge that his generosity entailed little in the way of real self-sacrifice. Thanks to his vast wealth, he noted that he and his family "will give up nothing we need or want by fulfilling this 99 percent pledge."[4] The people in Lara's study who received envelopes filled with cash were kind of like mini-Buffetts. They weren't counting on the unexpected windfall to meet their basic needs. Indeed, they used this extra cash to buy things like sushi and Starbucks coffee that fall closer to the realm of treats than of necessities. So, would spending on others promote happiness even for people who needed the money? To find out, let's go to East Africa.

Around the World

All the research we've described so far in this chapter was conducted in the United States and Canada, wealthy countries where the average person enjoys a standard of living that would be unimaginable to most people in human history, and in much of the world today. Would investing in others lead to happiness even in relatively poor countries, where people often struggle to make ends meet—where spending money on others may come at the expense of meeting one's own basic needs? In a recent experiment, a total of more than eight hundred people drawn from both Canada and the East African nation of Uganda reflected on a time when they had spent a small sum of their own money: $20 in Canada or 10,000 shillings in Uganda, roughly equivalent amounts in buying power.[5] In each country, some people were told to think about a time they spent that sum of money on themselves, while others thought about a time they'd spent money on someone else.

Canada and Uganda differ in almost every way imaginable, from history and religion to climate and culture, but most importantly, the two countries lie at opposite ends of the earth in terms of per capita income. Canada falls in the top 15 percent of the world's countries, Uganda in the bottom 15 percent. When faced with the same set of instructions while participating in the same experiment, individuals in the two countries recalled very different kinds of spending experiences. A young woman in Canada who had been asked to think about a time she spent money on someone else wrote:

> I went with my sister to buy a birthday present for my mom. We went to an accessory store in a mall to buy her a purple scarf. It was about $15 or so from Aldo Accessories.

Faced with the same set of instructions, a young woman in Uganda recalled:

> On Sunday, I was walking and met a longtime friend who was her son sick of malaria—the father has no money at the time, they left their home, she decided to visit a nearby clinic. I then ended giving her 10,000 [shillings] for medical bills and transport.

The first memory is a perfectly nice, familiar, instance of investing in others. This young woman probably hopped in her car, drove to the mall, bought the scarf, maybe grabbed a meal at the Cheesecake Factory, and headed home. But this memory couldn't be more different from the second one, in which a Ugandan woman sacrifices her money to save another person's life. Indeed, almost 15 percent of Ugandans reported spending on others in response to some negative event (often health-related), whereas this sort of spending was effectively nonexistent for Canadians.

That said, people are people. So there were also some striking similarities in the kinds of prosocial spending instances that people recalled. Consider this one from a young man in Uganda:

> I called a girl I wished to love. We went to peers joint and took 2 meals and one litre soda which totaled to 10,000, but however I did not achieve this girl up to now.

Again, the "10,000" is Ugandan shillings—roughly $20, which does seem a bit on the low end if he really hoped to "achieve" her. Compare it to this one, another romantically inclined young man, this time from Canada:

> I took my girlfriend out for dinner at a local restaurant for her birthday. We then went to a movie (which was so bad we left halfway through) and then went back to her room for . . .

Both you and this young Canadian fellow may have been hoping for a more interesting ending to that sentence than the real one: "cake." Like his Ugandan counterpart, he appears not to have "achieved" his girl up to now. Different cultures, similar forms of investing in others.

More importantly, the consequences for happiness were similar across Canada and Uganda. People in both countries felt happier after thinking about a time when they'd spent their own money on others rather than themselves. Investing in others promotes happiness, even in relatively impoverished countries where money is tight and where prosocial spending commonly entails helping someone in dire need rather than enjoying a pleasant trip to the mall.

Indeed, the link between prosocial spending and happiness is remarkably universal. Between 2006 to 2008, the Gallup World Poll surveyed representative samples of people in 136 countries, providing the clearest psychological snapshot to date of human life on Earth. More than two hundred thousand respondents answered scores of questions, including whether they had donated to charity in the past month and how satisfied they were with life.[6] And in 120 out of 136 countries, people who donated to charity in the past month reported greater satisfaction with life. This relationship emerged in poor and rich countries alike, and held up even after controlling for individuals' income. Across the 136 countries studied in the Gallup World Poll, donating to charity had a similar relationship to happiness as doubling household income.

So, unlike honeybee costumes for dogs, the emotional benefits of investing in others aren't simply a product of societies with excess cash. Rather, the proclivity to derive joy from investing in others might just be a fundamental component of human nature.

The Littlest Humans

If humans are predisposed to experience joy from giving, even young children might derive pleasure from donating their resources to others. As anyone who has ever tried to get a child to share anything with anyone knows, generosity does not always come easily to children. Could investing in others lead to happiness even for these tough customers?

In an experiment with twenty toddlers on the cusp of turning two, each tot met several puppets, who all happened to like Goldfish crackers and Teddy Grahams.[7] The experimenter gave each puppet one of these treats, and the puppets pretended to eat their treats by making "YUMMM" eating noises. Next, the toddlers met a new monkey puppet, aptly named Monkey, who they were told also loved treats. The toddlers got eight treats of their own, and then the fun began. The experimenter handed toddlers a treat from her own private stash and suggested that the child give it to Monkey. But then the experimenter asked toddlers to give one of their own precious treats to Monkey.

What made toddlers happiest? As you might guess, two-year-olds have a hard time filling out happiness scales, so the researchers coded the toddlers' facial expressions for spontaneous signs of happiness. How happy did they look? Toddlers looked pretty happy when they received eight treats for themselves. Critically, however, giving treats away to Monkey made toddlers happier than when they received treats for themselves. Perhaps most surprisingly, toddlers were happiest of all when they gave *their very own treat* to Monkey. Faced with the toddler equivalent of gold (Goldfish crackers), children derived more happiness from giving this precious resource away than from getting more of it themselves. And the impact of investing in others on happiness was biggest when giving was most costly—when the treat came from their personal stash.

Some parents may wonder if *their* children are in fact part wolf, and missed out on this lovely component of human nature. Sure, sometimes little Caitlin or Jimmy toddles up to you, offering you one of their Cheerios and breaking into a delighted smile when you accept. But other times, asking children to share results in Cheerio-soaked mayhem. Although the warm glow of giving can be detected in countries around the world and even among young children, these findings don't mean that people *always* experience pure, unmitigated happiness from helping others. It almost goes without saying that individuals differ in both their proclivity to share with others and the joy they experience from doing so. As a graduate student, Liz was frequently rebuffed when she attempted to take bites of food from the plate of her fully grown and otherwise charming boyfriend Benjamin (whom you may remember from chapter 2). Reflecting on his childhood, Ben's mother shook her head and explained sadly, "Benjamin just never liked to share."

Even leaving aside such individual differences, research shows that the nature of the giving situation matters. Investing in others can take a seemingly limitless variety of forms, from donating to a charity that helps strangers in a faraway country to buying lunch for a friend. When does giving promote the most happiness? Understanding the answer to this complex question can help us get the biggest happiness bang for our prosocial buck—and can help us create positive giving experiences for our children, clients, customers, and employees. Below, we describe three strategies designed to boost the impact of investing in others: Make It a Choice, Make a Connection, and Make an Impact.

Make It a Choice

Emily Smits, a former comedy writer, spent her early twenties working on busy street corners, canvassing passersby for charitable donations. Although she assured people that she didn't bite, Emily remembers one businessman who veered off the pavement just to avoid her, running into a parked car in his bid for escape.[8] Most of us have experienced a situation in which we felt cornered into providing help, whether by an overeager street canvasser, a colleague's child selling overpriced cakes for her Brownie pack, or a friend's awkward request for a loan (an event so ubiquitous that googling "awkward loan requests" gets about 90 million hits). Not surprisingly, feeling cornered can suck the joy out of giving. Over a two-week period, 138 university students kept a daily diary, reporting how they felt each day and whether they had helped someone else or done something for a worthy cause.[9] Students reported feeling better on days when they did something prosocial, but only when their actions felt self-chosen. If students helped because they felt like they had to or because people would be mad otherwise, they felt *worse* on days when they did good things.

The value of choice can also be seen in brain scans. In a study at the University of Oregon, researchers paid $100 to people who then donated some of this money to a food bank—all from the inside of a scanner that assessed brain activity as they donated.[10] Sometimes people could choose whether to give money, but sometimes the donations were mandatory, more like taxation. Even when donations were mandatory, giving to this worthwhile charity provoked activation in reward areas of the brain. But activation in these reward areas (along with self-reported satisfaction) was considerably greater when people *chose* to donate than when their prosocial spending was obligatory.

If you're a professional fund-raiser or you're participating in a Tough Mudder Run and gathering donations for its affiliated charity (the Wounded Warrior Project), maybe you should just set up a pretty website and then let people decide whether to donate of their own accord. There's just one problem with this strategy: you're not likely to collect much money. One of the most common reasons people report donating to charity is that someone asks them to give.[11] The trick, then, is to craft charitable appeals that encourage people to give, without making them feel forced to comply.

Even subtle changes in the nature of a request can make all the difference. In one study, a graduate student requested a bit of help and ended her plea by saying either, "It's entirely your choice whether to help or not" or "I really think you should help out."[12] In both cases, the personal plea was highly effective. More than 97 percent of people agreed to help. Importantly, though, helpers felt happier if they had been reminded that helping was their choice rather than being told they *should* help. What's more, people reminded of choice provided higher-quality assistance and felt a closer sense of connection with the person they helped.

Make a Connection

Dave Dawes, forty-seven, had been dating his girlfriend Angela for four years but had been holding off on getting married while they scraped together money for a wedding.[13] Then, in October 2011, a surprising thing happened: the British couple won £101 million.[14] With the winnings in hand, Dave promised Angie a new diamond engagement ring, and the couple looked forward to making their wedding "a bit more glamorous." And unlike some of those would-be lottery winners we quoted at the beginning of the book, they began to consider donating some of their winnings to worthy causes, particularly children's charities. But first they decided to turn their closest friends and family members into millionaires. Dave explained, "We've drawn up a list of 15 to 20 people . . . anyone who has helped us through our lives," promising each one a million pounds. (All the calls have now been made, so don't hold your breath if you haven't heard from them yet.) How did the lucky people on their list react? As Angie put it, "They are gobsmacked, amazed."[15]

Although Dave and Angie's act of generosity occurred on an unusually grand scale, their decision to prioritize friends and family carries through to the spending habits of those of us who have so far failed to win one of the world's largest lottery prizes. In the same week that the Daweses won the lottery, Americans told the Gallup organization that they planned to spend an average of more than $700 on Christmas gifts,[16] with the bulk of that spending typically targeted toward presents for friends and family.[17] Since gift givers pay more to purchase presents, on average, than the recipients themselves say they would be willing to pay for the same items, economist Joel Waldfogel has argued that Christmas creates a "deadweight loss" of at least $4 billion within the United States alone.[18]

But a straight-up economic analysis overlooks the critical role that gifts can play in strengthening relationships. Indeed, after learning that their girlfriends have selected a desirable gift for them, men in long-term relationships are significantly more likely to say that the relationship will continue—and end in marriage.[19] Not only that, but people derive more happiness from spending money on "strong ties" (such as significant others, but also close friends and immediate family members) than on "weak ties" (think a friend of a friend, or a step-uncle).[20]

Of course, your connection with the recipient of your gifts isn't all that matters. *How* you give it is important, too. To explore this idea, Lara decided to hand out $10 Starbucks gift cards.[21] She told some people to use the gift card to take someone else out for coffee at Starbucks. She told others to give the gift card away to someone else, but she insisted that they refrain from accompanying that person to Starbucks. So, people in both groups got the chance to invest in others, specifically through the gift of caffeination, but only one group was allowed to spend time with the beneficiary of their gift. Meanwhile, Lara handed out additional gift cards to a different group of lucky people, telling them to spend the gift card on themselves; half of these people went to Starbucks by themselves, while the others visited Starbucks with a friend but spent the card only on themselves. Who was happiest by the end of the day? The people who used the gift card to benefit someone else *and* who spent time with that person at Starbucks. Investing *and* connecting provided the most happiness. Think of your own prosocial spending budget in terms of levels of connection. You're likely to get the biggest happiness bang for your prosocial buck if you invest in others in ways that help you connect with people, especially people you care about.

But it's possible to create a sense of connection even with total strangers.[22] The idea for DonorsChoose.org (the charity which allowed Mike to donate his $50 Crate & Barrel voucher) came from the experience of founder Charles Best, a former state school teacher. Like many state school teachers, Charles found himself buying supplies for the students in his underfunded classroom.[23] One day he happened to mention his shopping trips to a (wealthier) friend, who offered to buy some supplies for Charles's class. Creating links between a specific donor and a specific classroom enables an emotional connection to emerge from what would otherwise be a cold financial transaction.

Today, the website Charles created gives potential donors enormous flexibility and agency in choosing which classroom to fund. People can search for a school in their home state, even search for a classroom in their old school, bringing the donation closer to home. Or they can adopt a different approach, giving based on their own interests (Mark Twain or microscopes). Or they can take still another approach, looking for the neediest classrooms regardless of the location of the school or the specific project posted by the teacher. Not only does DonorsChoose.org allow donors to make it a choice by investing in a specific group of students in a specific classroom, the site also creates the tangible, emotional connection often missing from the donation experience. And the connection doesn't end there. Teachers send thank-you notes to donors, and students themselves often send thank-you notes. "When we deliver the initial thank-you note to the donor, our first ask is not for money. Instead, we ask the donor to write back to the classroom, and we measure success in the volume of two-way correspondence that we see between donors and classrooms," Charles says.

Organizations like DonorsChoose.org make it easy for donors to see how their gifts make a difference. More broadly, when we meet friends at Starbucks and treat them to coffee, or foster a love of science in children, we witness the impact of our prosocial investments. As we'll see next, knowing that we're having an impact on someone else is another critical factor in transforming good deeds into good feelings.

Make an Impact

Kevin Starr, a physician in San Francisco, stumbled into the world of philanthropy. He was working in Bolivia with his friend and mentor Rainer Arnhold, when Rainer died unexpectedly. In the wake of his friend's death, Kevin learned more about Rainer's background. "He had a lovely family," Kevin explains, "and it turned out they'd been in banking for generations. And they were *very* good at it."[24] Rainer spent much of his life working to improve the lives of children living in poverty, and the family wanted to carry on that work. They asked Kevin to help them establish the Mulago Foundation, and he eventually became its managing director. Today, Kevin explains, the Mulago Foundation "looks for the best solutions to the biggest problems in the poorest countries."[25] In doing so, they "are unabashedly obsessed with impact: measuring it, funding it, and scaling it up." Before providing funding to an organization, Kevin's team at Mulago uses a rigorous system to evaluate potential impact, focusing not on optimistic platitudes from mission statements, but on measurable results.

All of us want our donations to have the kind of impact that Mulago assesses, but it can be difficult to see how our donation of £10 or £20 will make a difference. A donation to UNICEF (the United Nations Children's Fund) helps children around the world. There is no denying the importance of this cause, but it can be hard to see how a small donation to such a large, nebulous organization will make a concrete difference in a child's life. Contrast that with Spread the Net, which allows donors to contribute $10 to send one malaria net to sub-Saharan Africa. Their slogan? "A child dies needlessly from malaria every minute. One bed net can protect up to five children for five years. 1 net. 10 bucks. Save lives."[26] Both UNICEF and Spread the Net are worthy organizations devoted to children's well-being, and the two are partners. But it's a lot easier to see how your donation to Spread the Net will make an impact. And when donors give money to Spread the Net, they get a bigger happiness bang for each buck than when they give money to UNICEF.[27]

The benefits of having an impact can filter into your professional life, as well. In a study of eighty-two fund-raisers responsible for soliciting multimillion-dollar donations for the University of North Carolina, individuals who agreed with statements such as "I feel that my work makes a positive difference in other people's lives" were less likely to experience emotional exhaustion at work.[28]

But it isn't always easy to see how organizations make a difference. Kevin points to Kickstart, which "makes and markets manual irrigation pumps that allow people to shift into higher-yield, higher-value crops."[29] According to Kevin, "they have real impact," enabling poor farmers to increase their income tenfold. Marketing such products is expensive, and "it costs Kickstart about $250 to get a pump into the hands of a family that will use it well." That may seem like a lot of money to help just one family, but Kevin explains that "it looks quite different when posed as 'You give us $250, and we'll get a family out of poverty—forever.'"

Enabling donors to see the specific impact of charitable initiatives carries a huge potential payoff. By maximizing the emotional benefits of giving, the strategy can make people more willing to behave generously in the future. A recent experiment shows that giving and happiness are mutually reinforcing, creating a positive feedback loop and providing empirical support for our favorite song from summer camp, "Happiness Runs in a Circular Motion." After reflecting on a time when they had spent money on themselves or others, students received an envelope filled with cash.[30] This time, though, they were allowed to *choose* how to spend their windfall. Not only did people feel happier after reflecting on a time when they spent money on others, but the happier they felt after thinking about their past spending experience, the more inclined they were to spend this new cash-filled envelope on others rather than themselves.

Is it possible to let people taste the joy of making a positive impact for as little as a dollar? It's tough to imagine how such a small donation could make a difference—unless you join forces with others. In 2012, Daniel Hawkins formed the Dollar Collective. Members each contribute $1, and the group decides what random act of generosity to perform with the pool of money.[31] As their first act, they surprised a young couple out for Valentine's Day and paid for their entire meal. Several members of the Dollar Collective witnessed the gift, and they caught the event on videotape to share with the rest of the group. And the couple who received the unexpected free meal? They decided to give the money they saved on dinner to a local charity (as well as buying some treats for their cat).[32]

When prosocial spending is done right—when it feels like a choice, when it connects us with others, and when it makes a clear impact—even small gifts can increase happiness, potentially spurring a domino effect of generosity.

Salivary Secrets

The benefits of investing in others don't stop at just making you feel happier. Giving your money away can make you physically healthier, and even make you feel financially wealthier. In a study of more than a thousand older adults, individuals who provided money and other forms of support to both relatives and nonrelatives reported better overall health. This relationship held after taking into account income, mobility, and other variables.[33] Although the health benefits of helping others likely compound over time, even a single instance of prosocial spending can have downstream consequences. In one experiment, people were paid $10 and told they could share as much or as little of their payment with another person (who hadn't received any money) as they wished.[34] Think about how much *you* would give, knowing that the other person has to accept what you give them and that there is no penalty for keeping the whole $10. In this experiment, people decided to give a little less than half of the $10 away—$4.48, to be exact. The more dollars people gave away, the happier they felt. People who gave more money also reported feeling less ashamed, presumably because hoarding a windfall comes with some social stigma.

Besides asking people to report how they were feeling, the researchers made a more unusual request. They asked everyone to chew lightly on a cotton roll called a Salivette (since we're sure we've whetted your appetite with that description, know that you can purchase some yourself from the Sarstedt company, out of Nümbrecht, Germany). Why make people chew cotton, other than to laugh at them when they try to speak? To measure their level of cortisol—a hormone linked to the experience of stress—which can be assessed via saliva.

As it turns out, the more shame people felt upon deciding how much money to keep for themselves, the higher the levels of cortisol in their saliva afterward, suggesting that generous or stingy economic decisions can get under the skin. Although a little spike in cortisol won't harm you, elevated levels of this stress hormone can cause wear and tear on the body over time. Cortisol has been linked to a variety of health problems, including heart disease.[35]

Remember the research that showed that giving time away can make you feel like you have more time? Giving money away has a parallel effect. People who report donating money to charity feel wealthier than those who do not, even controlling for how much money they make. And giving as little as $1 away can cause you to feel wealthier.[36] In one experiment, people received an envelope stuffed with $1 and were assigned to keep this money, donate the money to charity (picking a DonorsChoose.org project), or give the money back to the experimenter. Who *felt* wealthier? Logically, people who had to give the money back and people who gave it to charity should feel equally poor—they were both out a dollar. But people who gave the money away felt far wealthier than those who gave it back, to such an extent that they felt just as wealthy as people who'd gotten a free dollar. Just as being able to give time away makes us feel that we must have a lot of time to spare, giving money away makes us feel that we must have a lot of money.

Investing in others brings a host of benefits to the giver, affecting not only happiness, but also health and feelings of wealth. In the next section, we explore whether giving money away can not only make people *feel* wealthier, but also *create* wealth.

The Bottom Line

In 2009, Pepsi shocked the advertising world by announcing that the company was "punting" the Super Bowl. After a twenty-three-year run, Pepsi pulled all advertising for its trademark brands during the 2010 Super Bowl.[37] Instead, the company diverted its typical $20 million Super Bowl budget to support grants for a new cause-marketing program: the Pepsi Refresh Project. The program allowed people to submit ideas for grants to "refresh" their communities, and Pepsi awarded grants to ideas that generated the most votes. Amazingly, more votes were cast for Pepsi Refresh projects than had been cast in the 2008 U.S. presidential election. And by making the surprising decision *not* to advertise, Pepsi got more buzz than most companies that bought Super Bowl ads, piling on three hundred thousand new Facebook fans.

While the program was intended to engage Pepsi's consumers, the team at Pepsi noticed an additional, and emotionally powerful, effect on the engagement of their own employees. Ami Irazabal, a senior marketing director at Pepsi and the leader of the Pepsi Refresh Project, noted that "people who work on the other brands here at PepsiCo ask, 'Is there any way I can help?'" The brand team seeded a special contest among groups of PepsiCo's employees: Each group submitted an idea for a $10,000 grant, all employees got the chance to vote, and CEO Indra Nooyi announced the winner at a town-hall meeting. Internal research showed that 97 percent of employees felt that the project reinforced their pride in PepsiCo as a company. And Kristine Hinck, senior manager, Pepsi Beverages Company Communications, told us that one employee even wrote in to say, "In my 30 years as a PepsiCo employee, I've never been more proud!"[38]

In a more rigorous test of the benefits of prosocial spending, National Australia Bank gave a random subset of its employees 100 Australian dollars to donate to a charity of their choice, through the charity website karmacurrency.com.au.[39] After making the donation, these employees not only felt happier, but also reported increased job satisfaction on a follow-up survey.

Some companies are providing employees with opportunities to give not only to charitable causes, but also to one another. Laszlo Bock, vice president for people operations at Google, explains that "[a]ny employee can give any other employee $150" from a special fund.[40] "There's no oversight, no management review, no approvals required. The only requirement is that you have to write at least a sentence explaining why they got it." Even in a company that pays "aggressively" (as Laszlo puts it), where $150 represents a vanishing fraction of most employees' income, Google's research shows that this small bonus "is more effective—and makes people happier—than a cash-based award from a manager or executive."

Could small bonuses that allow team members to provide benefits to each other not only enhance the recipient's happiness, but also make the team as a whole more successful? To find out, researchers infiltrated a recreational dodge ball league.[41] On some teams, players received $20 and were told to spend the money on one of their teammates. On other teams, players were given $20 to spend on a bill, expense, or gift for themselves. Players who received a personal bonus bought things that dodge ball players (apparently) love, including juice, pitas, and a bottle of Dr. McGillicuddy's Fireball whiskey. Those who received a prosocial bonus also bought plenty of food and alcohol, but for others rather than just themselves.

And one person even bought a piñata for the team. Think of the difference between a team member buying himself some whiskey, versus a team member buying a piñata. (We picture the team smashing a brightly colored donkey until it exploded in a candy shower.) Did these prosocial bonuses improve team performance? Teams who had been given personal bonuses went from winning 50 percent of their games before they received the bonus to 43 percent after. But those teams who received prosocial bonuses went from winning 50 percent of their games to dominating the league, winning fully 80 percent of their games post-bonus.

Winning at dodge ball is one of the most important human endeavors, as we all know, but can prosocial bonuses benefit other organizations? Replicating the dodge ball study in a different context, researchers handed out money again, this time to fourteen pharmaceutical sales teams in Belgium.[42] Each team consisted of about eight members, and the researchers gave several members of each team 15 euros, measuring team sales performance before and afterward. On half the teams, members were instructed to spend the money on themselves, while on the other teams, they spent the money on their teammates. Sales performance remained flat on the teams where members spent the money on themselves, but sales shot up on teams that received prosocial bonuses. For every 15 euros given to team members to spend on themselves, the company got just 4.5 euros back—a net loss. Because sales failed to increase, personal bonuses were wasted money. In sharp contrast, for every 15 euros given to a team member to spend prosocially, the company reaped 78 euros.

It's important to take these studies with a serious grain of salt given the small number of teams examined, but the sheer size of the observed effects points to the value of questioning traditional assumptions about the best ways to reward employees. Companies have developed an impressive array of compensation schemes to motivate employees, ranging from pay-per-performance to commissions to end-of-year bonuses. The wide variety in such schemes masks a shared assumption: the best way to motivate employees is to reward them with money that they then spend on themselves. Providing employees with bonuses used for prosocial actions toward charities and coworkers offers a novel and potentially profitable alternative.

Encouraging employees to invest in others pays off. What about encouraging customers to do the same? Xavier Helgesen and Christopher "Kreece" Fuchs found a creative way to make some cash when they were students at the University of Notre Dame. They gathered their friends' used textbooks and sold them online, taking a cut of the proceeds. The two friends also decided that they wanted both to make money and to give back, by donating part of the proceeds from their sales to charity. This idea evolved into their company, Better World Books, an online seller of used books that donates a percent of all profits to reading-related charities such as Books for Africa and the National Center for Family Literacy. Better World Books follows the principle of creating a connection: while customers never meet the people whom their purchases helped, the site creates a close connection between a donor reading a book and knowing that a recipient somewhere in the world will get to read a book as well.

Indeed, creating this connection is a crucial part of the business model. The company calls it "completing the full circle." CEO David Murphy says that the company tries to "connect the dots" in customers' minds: "Donate my books to Better World Books, and then buy my books from Better World Books," knowing all along that each of these actions helps to benefit needy recipients.[43] Imagine how you'd feel about a car company that told you to buy a car from them, then give it back to them for free and buy another car, and keep doing this over and over. Yet this is exactly the Better World Books model, and it works because customers feel connected to a cause they value.[44]

Despite its popularity, cause marketing doesn't guarantee increased profitability and everlasting joy. If not executed well, allowing customers to donate to charity by buying regular consumer goods can backfire. In a field study, researchers set up a charity booth at the University of Michigan to collect money for the American Cancer Society.[45] On days when they simply asked passersby to donate their spare change to the cause, they collected a total of $52.27. On days when they asked for donations and invited people to buy a can of Red Bull for $2.50 with 50 cents going to charity, they sold 15 cans (yielding $7.50 for charity) and collected $10.55 in donations. The donation drive yielded three times as much money when people were asked simply to donate. The problem? Cause marketing efforts can "crowd out" direct charitable giving, making people feel as though they've already done their part by purchasing, even when a tiny fraction of the purchase price goes to charity. What's worse, because cause-related marketing can focus people on their own desires (what iPod do I want?) rather than on the impact of their donations (how will someone benefit from this money?), it can reduce the happiness people get from giving.[46]

Although cause marketing has been around since at least

the 1970s, rigorous research on the broader consequences of these initiatives is just beginning. And websites such as www.buylesscrap.org encourage consumers to donate directly to charity rather than spending money on charity-linked products. So, what's a socially responsible company to do? As a start, we would encourage companies to think about fostering the conditions that promote the warm glow of giving, structuring cause-marketing initiatives so that customers feel that they are making a choice to support the cause, that they are connected to the beneficiaries, and that they are making a real impact.

That's Obvious

While on his way to give a talk at the University of Alberta a few years back, Mike was forced, like all American visitors to Canada, to pass through customs. For whatever reason—perhaps Irish Catholic guilt that he must have done *something* wrong—Mike generally panics whenever questioned by customs agents. Worse still, Mike was sporting a ginormous beard and a shaved head, while his outdated passport photo showed a beardless Mike with a reasonably full head of hair. The customs agent looked at the photo, then at Mike, then the photo, then Mike again. As beads of sweat began to appear on Mike's bald head, the border guard decided to ask some questions.

Agent: Are you here for work or pleasure?
Mike: Work. No, pleasure! I mean, part work and part pleasure, you know, like some of each.
Agent: (long pause) And what line of work are you in?
Mike: I'm a professor.

Agent: (longer pause, examines Mike's homeless-person beard and ripped jeans) A professor, eh? Whereabouts?

Mike: Harvard Business School.

Agent: (after seemingly thirty-seven-minute pause, further inspection of photo, outfit, and beard) And you're headed to?

Mike: The University of Alberta. They invited me to give a talk in the Marketing Department.

Agent: (contemplating putting Mike in safe room) What's the talk about then?

Mike: It's about how spending money on others makes you happier than spending money on yourself.

Agent: (incredulous, now fully convinced Mike is making the whole thing up) Well, that's obvious!

Aside from highlighting Mike's latent social anxiety, this anecdote reveals something about the principle in this chapter. Don't we already know this? Our parents told us from the time we were children that we were supposed to be nice to other people and share. Does this principle warrant our attention, when a customs agent was so sure it was true that he couldn't believe anyone would want to hear Mike talk about it? Yes, actually. Like knowing we should exercise and eat well, then plopping ourselves on the couch to scarf down some nachos, being aware that we should invest in others doesn't mean we do so—or at least not as much as we could or should. Many people recognize that giving can feel good, at least in the abstract. But when we ask people to consider spending money today, most of them predict that they'll be happier if they spend that money on themselves rather than on others.[47]

What is the correct ratio of spending on ourselves to investing in others? Recall that the ratio in some surveys is more than 10 to 1. If your ratio was higher than that when we asked you to calculate it earlier, definitely consider investing more in others. Even if your ratio was lower, our guess is that throwing an extra £5 to a charity, a friend, or a coworker would improve your happiness more than shoving that cash in your pocket and using it to make a habitual purchase. We're not suggesting that giving all of your money away is wise. Again, money does increase happiness to some extent, especially when it moves you to a decent standard of living. As in the other chapters, though, we propose doing something different than you usually would with the £5 in your wallet. Here we suggest that sometimes—just *sometimes*—you think about what you could do with the money for someone else.

If you can't think of ways to invest in others, consider the creative example of an anonymous donor in Indianapolis. Her story echoes that of Marcia Fiamengo, the widowed Virgin Galactic astronaut. While Marcia made plans to go to the moon, the woman in Indianapolis made plans to go to Kmart. At the shop, she paid the layaway orders for as many as fifty random strangers. As a final gesture, she handed out $50 bills while leaving the shop. "She was doing it in the memory of her husband who had just died, and she said she wasn't going to be able to spend it and wanted to make people happy with it," a shop employee said. The woman only asked people to "remember Ben."[48]

Epilogue

Zooming Out

So, now you've seen the five principles of happy money. The principles we outlined should not be considered as independent from each other. You shouldn't *either* buy experiences *or* invest in others, but rather think about applying as many principles as you can in your daily spending. It's even possible to apply multiple principles with a single purchase. Remember, the goal is to wring the most happiness out of every £5: the more principles used, the more happiness.

As we saw in the last chapter, a Starbucks gift card provided the most happiness when people used it to buy coffee for someone else, while accompanying them to Starbucks—which allowed them not only to invest in others (chapter 5), but also to buy an experience (chapter 1), and change the way they spent their time that day (chapter 3). And in your daily life, you could knock off the other two principles by paying up front for the Starbucks card at the beginning of the week (chapter 4) and putting just enough money on the card to buy a basic coffee Monday through Thursday, but a Frappuccino on Friday—making that delicious dose of creamy caffeine a treat (chapter 2). And of course, if there's this much flexibility in changing how you spend money on coffee, think of the range of possibilities in applying our principles to a host of purchases in your life.

Seriously. Think about it. Here are the principles again:

1. Buy Experiences
2. Make It a Treat
3. Buy Time
4. Pay Now, Consume Later
5. Invest in Others

So let's zoom out—beyond Frappuccinos, if you can stand to leave them behind for a moment—and think about how a typical household spends its money. In 2010, according to the U.S. Bureau of Labor Statistics, the average American household (or technically, "consumer unit") earned about $62,000 before taxes and spent a total of around $48,000, on the following categories (numbers are rounded to the nearest $100):*

Housing	$16,500
Transportation	$7,700
Personal insurance & pensions	$5,300
Food (at home)	$3,600
All other expenditures	$3,400
Healthcare	$3,200
Food (away from home)	$2,500
Entertainment	$2,500
Apparel and Services	$1,700
Donations (e.g., charities, churches)	$1,600

* See http://www.bls.gov/opub/focus/volume2_number12/cex_2_12.htm#table1. You can see how these spending allocations compare to the United Kingdom, Canada, and Japan by visiting http://www.bls.gov/opub/focus/volume2_number16/cex_2_16.htm.

How would you alter spending within these categories, or the allocations across them, in line with the five principles of happy money? We ordered spending from most to least. You'll notice that the two largest categories—housing and transportation—are not particularly good sources of happiness (recall that buying bigger houses and nicer cars doesn't make us much happier, not to mention spending money on petrol for our interminable commutes). And you'll also notice that the category in which people report spending *least*, investing in others, is an excellent source of happiness. Don't get us wrong. We know it's unrealistic to take *all* of the money you spend on housing and transportation and reallocate it to experiences and donations. But remember, even small purchases can make a difference for our happiness on a given day. The question is not "Should I sell my house and give it all to the Red Cross?" but rather "Could I reallocate even just £5 a week from one category to another?"

And just as importantly as reallocating, think about where you could cut back without sacrificing much happiness. Although we've devoted this book to *spending* money, *saving* money can also boost happiness. Our genes play a powerful role in shaping our happiness levels—especially, it turns out, among wealthier individuals.[1] Why? It's a little like height. Our genes propel us toward a certain stature, but an impoverished environment can get in the way. Savings can buffer us from the unpleasant shocks of life on earth, providing a cushion that ensures we can bounce back and achieve the levels of happiness entwined in our DNA.

Unfortunately, merely resolving to save more money i not enough. Abstract savings goals have a big effect on i dividuals' *expectations* about how much they will spend, little bearing on how much money they end up spending.[2] Try this approach instead: For one week, keep track of all the money you spend. Rather than grouping your expenditures into the traditional categories used by the Bureau of Labor Statistics, try putting them into categories according to our five spending principles. Then take a close look at all the discretionary income you've spent that falls *outside* these categories—and see how much of it you can forgo the following week.

Spending Big

Thus far, we've focused our attention on changing the way two different kinds of budgets are spent—the budgets that individuals spend trying to maximize happiness, and the budgets that managers spend trying to maximize the happiness of employees and customers. Let's zoom out even further, and think about the biggest spenders of all: governments. The ways in which governments both collect and spend taxpayers' money, *and* encourage those taxpayers to spend their own money, can exert an enormous impact on happiness. Of course, government interest in the happiness of citizens is not an entirely new endeavor. The Founding
athers, after all, included "the pursuit of happiness" as one
ust three inalienable rights in the Declaration of Inde-
nce in 1776. More recently, King Jigme Singye Wang-
Bhutan called in 1972 for using "Gross National
" to assess his country's health, supplementing
on economic metrics such as gross domestic

Beyond Bhutan, interest in the capacity of governments to measure and promote the well-being of citizens has increased in recent years. While we were writing this book, a first-of-its-kind event took happiness to a global level: As mandated by the United Nations General Assembly, the first United Nations Conference on Happiness took place on April 2, 2012. And policy makers—from the Behavioural Insights Team at 10 Downing Street to government officials in the small city of Somerville, Massachusetts—are assessing and attempting to increase the happiness of us regular folks.

Having Money to Spend

The first, glaringly obvious way governments can facilitate citizens' ability to spend their money in happier ways is to ensure that all citizens have *some* disposable income to spend in the first place. Traditionally, governments pursue this goal by striving to promote economic growth—the rising tide lifting all boats—but as psychologist David Myers notes, the rising tide has lifted "the yachts more than the dinghies" in recent years.[4] This growing chasm between the yachts and the dinghies has become a pressing political issue in the United States and around the world.

Take a quick, two-question quiz.

1. What percentage of all the wealth in the United States do you think the richest 20 percent of Americans own?
2. What percentage of the wealth do you think the poorest 40 percent of Americans own?

Got your guesses? The answers: the richest 20 percent own around 85 percent of the wealth and the poorest 40 percent own approximately 0 percent.[5] That's not a typo. The bottom two-fifths of Americans have vanishingly close to *none* of the country's total wealth, while the top 20 percent have nearly all of it. In short, if people need some disposable income to start spending it in happier ways, we're far from fulfilling this basic prerequisite.

There is good news, though. But before we get there, answer two related but different questions. This time there are no right or wrong answers. We just want your beliefs about the ideal America.

1. What percentage of the wealth do you think the richest 20 percent of Americans *should* own?
2. What percentage of the wealth do you think the poorest 40 percent of Americans *should* own?

According to a recent survey of some five thousand Americans, people in the United States would ideally like the richest 20 percent of Americans to own 32 percent of the wealth and the poorest 40 percent to own 25 percent.[6] In other words, Americans *welcome* some wealth inequality. Rich people can be rich, poor people can be poor. But they'd like rich people to be less rich and poor people to have some money to spend. More remarkably, Americans—Republicans and Democrats, rich and poor—show remarkable consensus in their desired distribution of wealth. *Everyone* wants poor people to have more than they currently have and rich people to have less than they do now. The good news for giving everyone the chance to spend happier money? These results suggest that Americans broadly support more equal distributions of wealth. But *not* completely equal, for readers who are concerned about the potential negative effects of too much equality on overall economic growth.

And Americans appear to be on to something. More even distributions of income are associated with greater happiness. Looking beyond the United States, research shows that a more equal distribution of money across people is associated with higher average well-being in the world's countries.[7] In one survey of more than fifty-nine thousand respondents from fifty-four countries, people in wealthier countries (as assessed by per capita gross domestic product) were generally happier than people in poor countries. That's not that surprising. However, even when controlling for the wealth of nations, the more *unequal* the distribution of income, the lower well-being people reported on average. In other words, whether countries were rich or poor, their inhabitants' happiness depended on the relative disparities in their incomes.* Why would this be? Some research suggests that inequality is associated with other behaviors linked to unhappiness. As inequality increases in a country, that country's poor experience relatively greater financial distress compared to the poor in less unequal countries. And as financial distress increases, so do divorce rates and commute times—as poorer people move farther from their places of work in an effort to find cheaper housing.[8] It

* Interestingly, the link between inequality and happiness *within* a country varies substantially. For example, the happiness of Europeans is more closely tied to inequality than the happiness of Americans—perhaps because Americans believe (erroneously) that they have more of an opportunity to rise in the income distribution. See Alberto Alesina, Rafael Di Tella, and Robert MacCulloch, "Inequality and happiness: Are Europeans and Americans different?," *Journal of Public Economics* 88, no. 9/10 (August 2004): 2009; and Lisa A. Keister, *Getting Rich: America's New Rich and How They Got That Way* (New York: Cambridge University Press, 2005).

is perhaps not surprising, then, that countries with stronger social safety nets tend to be happier, as well.[9]

Taken together, these findings suggest that people are happier in countries with more equal distributions of income. Even in countries like the United States, where wealth distributions are more unequal, most people believe that most people should have some money to spend. Of course, ensuring that people *have* some disposable income is a necessary but not sufficient condition for people to maximize their happiness when they spend it. Assuming—and it's a big assumption—that people *do* have some money, how can governments encourage them to spend that money in happier ways?

More Money, Fewer Problems?

There's a puzzle that's plagued psychologists, economists, and policy makers for decades. Governments strive to promote economic growth with the assumption that doing so will enhance their constituents' well-being (and, hey, maybe get them reelected). Interestingly, though, the data are mixed as to whether citizens get any happier as their country gets richer.[10] One intriguing trend emerges from the data, however: economic growth appears to do more for the happiness of the average citizen in some countries (like Denmark, the Netherlands, and Italy) than in others (like the United States and China).[11] Alan Krueger, tapped by President Obama to be chairman of the White House Council of Economic Advisers, suggests that this variation poses a pressing new puzzle: "Why do some countries do a much better job translating income gains into happiness than others?"[12]

If the amount of happiness your money buys depends on how you spend it, might the same idea hold true at the level of countries? The variability in how governments choose to spend money, and encourage their citizens to spend their own money, may explain why some countries are so skilled at turning cash into happiness. Unlike individuals, countries rarely sign up for psychology experiments. Because we can't draw strong causal conclusions until we convince countries to do so, discussing these differences between countries is best considered as a thought exercise—for now. And we should also note that our focus is on the impact of changing policies specifically on people's *happiness.* When we suggest below that it may not be wise for governments to encourage rampant home ownership, our focus is on the happiness of individual homeowners, and *not* the additional macroeconomic consequences.

Buy Experiences

What caused the economic crisis in the United States in 2008? Opinions vary, of course, but most people point to the collapse of the housing bubble—in conjunction with subprime mortgages—as a key contributor. While the respective contributions of government agencies like Fannie Mae and Freddie Mac and the private lenders issuing subprime mortgages will be debated for decades, one driver of the bubble is clear: Americans are propelled to buy houses, and take on debt and risk to own one. (Recall that some 90 percent of Americans link home ownership to living the American dream.)[13]

In Canada, unlike the United States, mortgage lenders

have full recourse to the borrower's assets and income, and mortgage interest is not tax-deductible.[14] These differences between two otherwise similar countries offer a stark contrast. Americans are encouraged to buy houses with incentives such as protection of their other assets and tax benefits, incentives unavailable to Canadians. One of the largest material purchases people ever make is their home, yet home purchases usually fail to make people any happier. By encouraging people to buy houses, the United States government implicitly encourages people to buy stuff. By reducing incentives for home buying, the Canadian government decreases that temptation.

If governments encourage citizens to buy less stuff (like houses), should they also institute policies to encourage the pursuit of experiences instead? Evidence from the city of Somerville, Massachusetts—just north of Mike's home in Cambridge—suggests yes. The city asked more than six thousand residents to rate their satisfaction with various aspects of life in Somerville, from traffic to schools to snow removal (a big deal, given Massachusetts winters). The goal? The city wanted to determine what aspects of life in Somerville exerted the greatest influence on inhabitants' happiness. As it turned out, residents' ratings of "the appearance and maintenance of parks" and "the beauty or physical setting of the city" were important predictors of their overall happiness with Somerville.[15] It's easier for people to seek out experiences, from picnics in the park to nights on the town, when the local environment provides appropriate settings.

Governments often provide support for museums, national parks, and other cultural institutions, thereby making experiential purchases accessible and affordable for their citizens. To *experience* those experiences, of course, people need to have the time to pursue them. And countries vary not just in providing more kinds of experiences, but in the amount of "free time" their inhabitants have, particularly in the form of government-mandated holiday days. In Denmark, ranked among the world's happiest countries, the Danish Holiday Act requires that workers get five paid weeks off each year,[16] leaving the Danes with more time for experiences than people have in countries such as the United States, which lacks a mandatory holiday requirement.[17,*]

Make It a Treat

Applying comedian Sarah Silverman's mantra to the governance of nation-states is far from straightforward. Governments are in the business of making sure people have the opportunity to get what they most want, whereas "making it a treat" is all about limiting the supply of our favorite things. We're in uncharted territory here, since we can't help but love big-box stores and special deals that help us get more, more, more—especially with those magic words: "Buy One, Get One Free."

David Halpern, director of the Behavioural Insights Team in the British Government explains, "We know that 'Buy One, Get One Free' drives up consumption very substantially, particularly for some product classes."[18] As David notes, these deals aren't a problem when they allow us to stock up on

---

[*] Of course, working less can mean less money to spend for individuals and at a macroeconomic level, less economic growth. Nor does more time off necessarily mean people will choose to follow the buy-experiences principle. Still, providing people with opportunities to buy experiences *and* ensuring they have some time to follow through may be wise, given the positive effects of buying experiences on happiness.

toothpaste, soap, and other necessities, while saving us some money along the way. After all, necessities like these have an important property: we can only use so much of them. It's rare for people to overconsume toothpaste. We brush a couple of times a day, and that's that. Things get more complicated when we get deals on things that we *are* prone to overconsume, like chocolate or alcohol. In these cases, "Buy One, Get One Free" doesn't just save us money. It can also negatively affect our physical health. From the happy money perspective, deals like these also introduce a potential problem for our *emotional* health. As many of us know all too well, whether there are one, two, or ten chocolates in front of us, we scarf them down as fast as we can, potentially undermining our enjoyment of each confection.

Should governments ration how much chocolate we eat? It sounds crazy, we admit. Except that governments implicitly ration all kinds of products we consume, via taxation. Consider cigarette taxes: In 2011, Missouri had the lowest state cigarette excise tax in the United States—just $0.17 per pack—while New York's was more than *twenty-five times* higher, at $4.35 per pack.[19] And as you might expect, taxes are related to consumption. New York has lower rates of smoking than Missouri, and in general, states with higher taxes tend to have fewer smokers.[20]

Nor are taxes the only way that governments can encourage us to make things a treat. Many regions have laws that limit the sale of alcohol to certain times and places. Interestingly, however, the trend has been to increase rather than decrease access to alcohol. Take the Orwellian-titled Restaurant Rejuvenation Act, passed in Massachusetts in 2010. The cornerstone of the act was the so-called brunch exception, which permitted restaurants to serve liquor starting at 10 A.M. on Sundays, two hours earlier than the previous noon start.[21] We love mimosas as much as anyone, but changes in policy that increase access to alcohol may decrease the likelihood that people take breaks from it, making alcohol less of a treat.

Alcohol is a traditional vice, but sugary sodas are the latest bad boys of the beverage world. Policies banning the vending machines that dispense them are spreading in American schools. The first was passed in Arkansas in 2003.[22] The evidence is mixed on the effect of such bans on childhood obesity and on children's health more broadly.[23] But banning soda for a large chunk of the day may have an additional benefit, restoring children's enjoyment of drinks best regarded as treats.

Of course, smokers and drinkers aren't always thrilled about policies that tax cigarettes or limit access to alcohol and soda. (Mike admits that he might take to the streets if Massachusetts tried to limit his access to Diet Coke.) But these examples show that governments can encourage people both to limit and break up consumption with simple policy changes.

Buy Time

Commuting times show enormous variability between countries, ranging from a low of around 25 minutes each way in Ireland and Denmark (oh that Denmark!) to more than 50 minutes each way in Korea and South Africa.[24] Governments are quite adept at altering how much time and money people spend commuting, with both carrots and sticks. First, the sticks. Cities from

London to Milan to Singapore have begun charging higher tolls to use heavily trafficked roads at the times when those roads are most likely to be congested. (A similar initiative failed to pass in New York City.) While the heavier burden such congestion pricing places on poorer commuters must be considered, at their best such initiatives would encourage people not only to avoid being stuck in traffic, but also to seek out alternative means of shortening their commutes.

Now for the carrots: Consider an innovative program launched by Washington, D.C.'s Office of Planning called Live Near Your Work.[25] The program offers up to $12,000 in incentives for people who move within two miles of work, half a mile of the subway, or a quarter mile to a bus stop. And in London, for an annual fee of £90 you can access bikes stashed at any one of the dozens of Barclays Cycle Hire stands around the capital city, for up to half-an-hour at a time for no extra charge, making biking as convenient and affordable as sitting on a bus or taking the tube.

Okay, so you don't live in London. In that case, consider buying a bike. Think biking instead of driving will take too long? Nearly 22 percent of all car rides in the UK are two miles or less and about 56 percent are five miles or less,[26] a reasonable distance for a bike ride (especially considering time typically spent stuck in traffic).

As with commuting times, countries vary widely in preferred modes of transportation. The percentage of trips taken that use public transportation, walking, and biking range from 14 percent in Australia and a low of 11 percent in the United States (yes, 89 percent of trips in the United States are by car) to a whopping 67 percent in Latvia and 52 percent in the Netherlands (a statistic that won't surprise tourists who've nearly been demolished by the hordes of cyclists in Amsterdam). These rates are negatively correlated with obesity, as we might expect given that walking and biking require more effort than sitting in an SUV.[27]

But would encouraging biking increase happiness? Within American cities, the percentage of commuters who cycle to work is positively correlated with average happiness in those cities (though cities with lots of bikers also have a higher standard of living in general, which may account for at least some of the effect).[28] Time spent driving is a bust for happiness, whereas time spent exercising is a boon. Taking a bike to work (even once a week) can transform our happiness-wasting commuting time into happiness-inducing physical activity time. Governments can help make this happen.

Pay Now, Consume Later

In the United States, the income tax system is structured such that many people overpay during the year and then receive a tax refund when April rolls around. Doug Shulman, the commissioner of the Internal Revenue Service, notes that "80 percent of Americans get an average of a $3,000 refund."[29] Overpaying can have real costs, depriving people of the interest they could have earned on that money if they invested it during the year. In the United Kingdom, in contrast, the tax collection system is designed to minimize error, such that relatively few people end up receiving tax refunds (or owing money) at the end of the year.

At first glance, the British system sounds great. But consider the consequences if the British system were skewed toward overcollecting taxes during the year so that people very rarely have to make a repayment at the end of the year. What would happen instead? Many people receive a rebate, more similar to standard operating procedure in countries like the United States. How would this policy help taxpayers follow our principle to pay now and consume later? Overcollection helps ensure that people pay up front rather than devoting all their dough to immediate consumption and then being left short-handed when the tax bill is due.

Whether in the market for a new car, a new television, or a new house, phrases like "no money down" and "no payments for 24 months" are featured up front, with the gory details of how payments can balloon over time buried in the small print. While people disagree about many aspects of the newly created U.S. Consumer Financial Protection Bureau, one goal of the agency is crystal clear: to help consumers understand what they are getting into with "deals" like these. By bringing the delayed costs to the forefront, the Consumer Financial Protection Bureau stands to counter the drive to consume now and pay later, by making the enormous potential "later" payments salient in the "now." The proposed new forms for home loans or mortgage refinancing, for example, include a single-page summary of key terms, including simple "Yes" or "No" responses as to whether monthly payments can increase and whether the loan has balloon payments. This information was included in previous forms but was often hidden deeper in the documents.[30] Government actions ranging from tipping the balance of tax collection to introducing new agencies can shape people's tendencies to pay now and consume later.

Invest in Others

Since countries with more equal distributions of income also tend to be happier countries, and people (at least in the United States) prefer more equal distributions of wealth, should governments follow their citizens' wishes to ensure that all of us have happy money to spend? One common method is via one of the least happy words of all—taxes. Not everyone hates higher taxes, however. Our "invest in others" guru Warren Buffett has noted that it is ludicrous that he should pay a lower rate of taxes on his vast wealth than his secretary does. In an editorial in the *New York Times*, he argued for higher taxes on the wealthy.[31] President Barack Obama has picked up on Buffett's advice, calling for the enactment of the "Buffett Rule," a minimum level of tax on the wealthiest Americans. To make the Buffett connection clear, he seated Buffett's secretary Debbie Bosanek in Michelle Obama's box for his 2012 State of the Union address.[32]

Despite these reasonable arguments, most of us are not thrilled about the idea of paying higher taxes. Commentaries on the topic include a blog titled "I Hate Income Tax: Seven Reasons to Remove the Greatest Evil Facing Americans"[33] and an "I Hate Taxes" Facebook fan page with the slogan "If you love freedom, then you hate taxes."[34] Research shows, however, that people in countries with more progressive taxation (like Sweden and Japan) are happier than those in countries where taxes are less progressive (like Italy and Singapore).[35] Given the benefits of progressive taxation, is there any way to make people happier paying their taxes? Think back to research showing that donations to a food bank elicited more activation in brain regions associated with reward when the contributions were made by choice rather than being obligatory.[36] Recent research offers a solution to the "I Hate Taxes" problem based on a similar principle. If we make taxes feel more like charitable contributions, people may be happier about having to pay them.

In a recent experiment, a national sample of more than four hundred Americans indicated their tax filing status and their income and then learned their marginal tax rate (their tax bracket).[37] Some respondents next completed a series of questions asking them to rate both the satisfaction they derived from paying their income taxes and the extent to which they felt their tax dollars provided benefits and paid for valuable services. Others first saw each of the categories in the federal budget—from military spending to antipoverty programs—and were asked to think about where, if given the option, they would most want to allocate 10 percent of their income tax. By adding an element of choice, this simple exercise increased both people's satisfaction with paying their taxes and their beliefs that their tax money provided value to the country. President Obama took a step in this direction in his 2011 State of the Union speech when he promised that, for the first time ever, American taxpayers could see how their federal tax dollars were spent (you can try it yourself at http://www.whitehouse.gov/2011-taxreceipt). The same experiment, though, also showed that merely *learning* where tax dollars were allocated did not change people's tax attitudes. Only being allowed to allocate money did the trick. You may be familiar from past tax returns with the only allocation U.S. citizens are currently allowed: designating just one of their tax dollars to the Federal Election Commission to finance presidential elections. We would suggest upping the ante from $1 to a more sizable chunk of income.*

* Note that people in the study were asked to consider how they would allocate only 10 percent of their total tax dollars. Increasing the level to 100 percent might cause necessary but boring services to become severely underfunded (who wants to pay for

How much do Americans care about investing in others? The United States has lower income taxes than many similar countries. Top earners paid a tax rate of 35 percent in 2011, compared to 50 percent in the United Kingdom and 52 percent in the Netherlands.[38] On the other hand, the United States is consistently in the top ten countries in the world in terms of percentage of citizens donating to charity. An impressive 65 percent of Americans reported donating money to charity in 2011, which in the end, is really just redistribution under another guise.[39] Through the power of allocation, the same people who loathe redistribution of income in the form of taxes may be perfectly willing to pay those taxes, provided that they have some choice in the matter, allowing them to reap the happiness benefits of investing in others.

The high rate of giving among Americans is due in part to another government decision that changes the frequency with which people invest in others: tax incentives for giving. Countries vary on whether charitable contributions can be deducted from income taxes, estate taxes, or both, and on the ceiling they set for total deductions. These policies are linked to the frequency with which people give.[40] Stronger incentives for giving have the potential to encourage greater investment in others.

Teach a Man to Spend . . .

We often get asked why people can't just figure out, through trial and error, which purchases make them happy, and

---

sewer maintenance when you could direct your donations to early childhood education?). Importantly, though, these results suggest that even having a say in just one out of every ten dollars can suffice to increase tax satisfaction.

which don't. One important reason, we believe, is that people just don't have the data they need. They don't fill out a happiness scale every day, then look back at the results and see what made them happy and unhappy that day. We get some feedback—we feel happy when eating cake, for instance—but this immediate feedback may not provide us with the right kind of data to maximize our happiness. It's not that human beings are incapable of using scales to understand themselves. We're all accustomed to weighing ourselves on scales, and we know that how much we eat and exercise makes our weight on that scale go up and down. Can we do the same with happiness?

This question brings us to a final tool that governments have at their disposal: raising awareness. Our principles show readers of this book the very best ways to spend money to reap the most happiness from every pound. Governments can provide such "happiness education" on a much broader scale. David Halpern offers this goal as his core job description: "Deshroud for citizens what it is that impacts their well-being, including their consumption choices."

And for libertarian-minded readers horrified at some of the government interventions we outlined in the previous sections, raising awareness offers a middle ground. Governments can provide accurate information on the determinants of well-being and then leave it up to citizens to decide how best to implement that knowledge in their own choices. David noted that the big question is whether making such data public "would affect market choices." For example, "Would people choose to live in a different area because reams of data show that people are happier there?" In the longer term, we can imagine that people would use their knowledge about the determinants of well-being to pressure governments to enact policies that maximize their own well-being. (This might have another happiness benefit: countries with democratic institutions—like direct election of politicians—tend to have happier citizens.)[41]

We told you earlier about the first ever United Nations Conference on Happiness in April 2012. The result of this endeavor? The 158-page *World Happiness Report*, which gathered the most cutting-edge thinking about happiness into one volume (full disclosure: one of the volume's co-editors, John Helliwell, is a collaborator of ours).[42] The goal? To provide a "how to" guide for policymakers interested in understanding how to measure and increase happiness. At a minimum, the report was successful at raising awareness of happiness in some countries that had not paid much attention previously. When several China-based news outlets reposted the report, the Chinese State Council Information Office—apparently not happy that China was ranked as the world's 112th happiest country—banned publishing or even *referring* to the report.[43] The report is just the start of bringing attention to happiness and starting a broader conversation. "We're really at the beginning," says David Halpern.

Can Happiness Be Bought?

Changing the way you spend your money is far from the *only* way to increase your happiness, of course.* But our principles show that money can do a much better job of buying you

* For a discussion of factors other than spending decisions that shape happiness, see Daniel Gilbert, *Stumbling on Happiness;* Sonja Lyubomirsky, *The How of Happiness;* or Jonathan Hadit, *The Happiness Hypothesis.* For a broader perspective on the role of government in shaping happiness, see John F. Helliwell, "How Can Subjective Well-being Be Improved?," http://www.csls.ca/festschrift/Helliwell.pdf.

happiness if you spend it right, since some purchases give you a bigger happiness bang for your buck than others. Still, though, is it wise to go around chasing happiness in your daily life? Isn't chasing happiness a bit of a fool's errand, a form of tilting at windmills? As a satirical headline from the *Onion* put it: "Grown Adult Actually Expects to Be Happy."[44] Some research suggests that chasing happiness can be counterproductive. People who were told to try to make themselves feel as happy as possible while they listened to some pretty good, but not fantastic music reported feeling less happy than those who hadn't been given any instructions.[45] It's hard to *will* yourself to be happier, as anyone who has been depressed knows. Being told to "just cheer up" is similar to being told to "just win a marathon." It's possible in theory, but a lot of help and practice is required. As we said at the outset, trying to get happier is like trying to conduct a heart transplant on yourself. Most of us could benefit from some expert guidance.

We selected the five principles in this book not only because each one is supported by rigorous research, but also because many of us—including the two of *us*—don't always follow them. Why? Because we mistakenly believe that we're *already* spending money in ways that will make us happier—the flat-screen TV and enormous house in the suburbs just *feel* like they'll provide lasting happiness. So, one likely reason why people's efforts to try to get happy often fail is, well . . . it's just not easy to figure it out. Each of our principles offers a scientifically validated means of increasing happiness. Like surgical experts performing a heart transplant, we're pretty confident that following these principles might be better than just winging it. And luckily, spending money is a lot easier and much less messy than major surgery.

Now, go out and try it for yourself. Spending happy money, we mean. Not performing a heart transplant.*

* Elizabeth Dunn and Michael Norton are not responsible for any complications arising from self-performed organ transplants.

Notes

Prologue

1. Elizabeth Landau, "Winning the Lottery: Does It Guarantee Happiness?," *CNN*, January 7, 2011, http://www.cnn.com/2011/HEALTH/01/07/lottery.winning.psychology/index.html.
2. Lara B. Aknin, Michael I. Norton, and Elizabeth W. Dunn, "From Wealth to Well-Being? Money Matters, but Less than People Think," *Journal of Positive Psychology* 4, no. 6 (November 2009): 523–27.
3. Ed Diener, Weiting Ng, James Harter, and Raksha Arora, "Wealth and Happiness across the World: Material Prosperity Predicts Life Evaluation, Whereas Psychosocial Prosperity Predicts Positive Feeling," *Journal of Personality and Social Psychology* 99, no. 1 (July 2010): 52–61.
4. Daniel Kahneman and Angus Deaton, "High Income Improves Evaluation of Life but Not Emotional Well-Being," *Proceedings of the National Academy of Sciences of the United States of America* 107, no. 38 (2010): 16489–93.
5. Paul K. Piff, Daniel M. Stancato, Stéphane Côté, Rodolfo Mendoza-Denton, and Dacher Keltner, "Higher Social Class Predicts Increased Unethical Behavior," *Proceedings of the National Academy of Sciences of the United States of America* 109, no. 11 (March 2012): 4086–91; Kathleen D. Vohs, Nicole L. Mead, and Miranda R. Goode, "Merely Activating the Concept of Money Changes Personal and Interpersonal Behavior," *Current Directions in Psychological Science* 17, no. 3 (June 2008): 208–12.
6. Kathleen D. Vohs, Nicole L. Mead, and Miranda R. Goode, "The Psychological Consequences of Money," *Science* 314, no. 5802 (November 2006): 1154–56.
7. Jenny Pennington, Dalia Ben-Galim, and Graeme Cooke, "No place to call home: The social impacts of housing undersupply on young people," Institute for Policy Research, http://www.ippr.org/images/media/files/publication/2012/12/no-place-home_Dec2012_10017.pdf:24.

8. Warren Buffett, "My Philanthropic Pledge," *CNNMoney*, June 16, 2010, http://money.cnn.com/2010/06/15/news/newsmakers/Warren_Buffett_Pledge_Letter.fortune/index.html.
9. For accessible reviews, see Daniel M. Wegner, *The Illusion of Conscious Will* (Cambridge, MA: MIT Press, 2002); Timothy D. Wilson, *Strangers to Ourselves: Discovering the Adaptive Unconscious* (Cambridge, MA: Belknap Press, 2002).

Chapter One. Buy Experiences

1 Naoki Nakazato, Ulrich Schimmack, and Shigehiro Oishi, "Effect of Changes in Living Conditions on Well-Being: A Prospective Top-Down Bottom-Up Model," *Social Indicators Research* 100, no. 1 (January 1, 2011): 115–35.
2. Elizabeth W. Dunn, Timothy D. Wilson, and Daniel T. Gilbert, "Location, Location, Location: The Misprediction of Satisfaction in Housing Lotteries," *Personality and Social Psychology Bulletin*29, no. 11 (2003): 1421–32.
3. David Streitfield, "Despite Fears, Owning Home Retains Allure, Poll Shows," *New York Times*, June 29, 2011, http://www.nytimes.com/2011/06/30/business/30poll.html.
4. Grace Wong Bucchianeri, "The American Dream or the American Delusion? The Private and External Benefits of Homeownership," working paper, University of Pennsylvania, 2011.
5. Author interview with Marcia Fiamengo, August 4, 2011.
6. Leaf Van Boven and Thomas Gilovich, "To Do or to Have? That Is the Question," *Journal of Personality and Social Psychology* 85, no. 6 (2003): 1193–1202.
7. Leonardo Nicolao, Julie R. Irwin, and Joseph K. Goodman, "Happiness for Sale: Do Experiential Purchases Make Consumers Happier Than Material Purchases?," *Journal of Consumer Research* 36, no. 2 (2009): 188–98.
8. Thomas DeLeire and Ariel Kalil, "Does Consumption Buy Happiness? Evidence from the United States," *International Review of Economics* 57, no. 2 (2010): 163–76.
9. Author interview with Will Dean, July 8, 2011.
10. Tough Mudder, http://toughmudder.com.
11. Ryan T. Howell and Graham Hill, "The Mediators of Experiential Purchases: Determining the Impact of Psychological Needs Satisfaction and Social Comparison," *Journal of Positive Psychology* 4, no. 6 (2009): 511–22.
12. John Branch, "Playing with Fire, Barbed Wire and Beer," *New York Times*, April 28, 2010, http://www.nytimes.com/2010/04/29/sports/29mudder.html.

13. Greg Perkins, "Tough Mudder: Dirty, Adventurous Fun!," *Modern Paleo*, October 25, 2010, http://blog.modernpaleo.com/2010/10/tough-mudder-dirty-adventurous-fun.html.
14. Leaf Van Boven, Margaret C. Campbell, and Thomas Gilovich, "Stigmatizing Materialism: On Stereotypes and Impressions of Materialistic and Experiential Pursuits," *Personality and Social Psychology Bulletin* 36, no. 4 (April 2010): 551–63.
15. Travis J. Carter and Thomas Gilovich, "I Am What I Do, Not What I Have: The Differential Centrality of Experiential and Material Purchases to the Self," *Journal of Personality and Social Psychology* (2012).
16. Ibid.
17. Gal Zauberman, Rebecca K Ratner, and B. Kyu Kim, "Memories as Assets: Strategic Memory Protection in Choice over Time," *Journal of Consumer Research* 35, no. 5 (2009): 715–28.
18. Tim Wildschut, Constantine Sedikides, Clay Routledge, Jamie Arndt, and Filippo Cordaro, "Nostalgia as a Repository of Social Connectedness: The Role of Attachment-Related Avoidance," *Journal of Personality and Social Psychology* 98, no. 4 (2010): 573–86.
19. Clay Routledge, Jamie Arndt, Tim Wildschut, Constantine Sedikides, Claire M. Hart, Jacob Juhl, Ad J. J. M. Vingerhoets, and Wolff Schlotz, "The Past Makes the Present Meaningful: Nostalgia as an Existential Resource," *Journal of Personality and Social Psychology* 101, no. 3 (2011): 638–52.
20. Fred Davis, "Nostalgia, Identity and the Current Nostalgia Wave," *Journal of Popular Culture* 11, no. 2 (1977): 414–24.
21. Anat Keinan and Ran Kivetz, "Productivity Orientation and the Consumption of Collectable Experiences," *Journal of Consumer Research* 37, no. 6 (2011): 935–50.
22. Ibid.
23. *Hercules Furens* (The Madness of Hercules), lines 656–57; *Amphitryon.*
24. W. Richard Walker and John Skowronski, "The Fading Affect Bias: But What the Hell Is It For?," *Applied Cognitive Psychology* 23 (2009): 1122–36.
25. Terence R. Mitchell, Leigh Thompson, Erika Peterson, and Randy Cronk, "Temporal Adjustments in the Evaluation of Events: The 'Rosy View,'" *Journal of Experimental Social Psychology* 33, no. 4 (1997): 421–48.
26. Derrick Wirtz, Justin Kruger, Christie Napa Scollon, and Ed Diener, "What to Do on Spring Break? The Role of Predicted, On-line, and Remembered Experience in Future Choice," *Psychological Science* 14, no. 5 (September 2003): 520–24.
27. Travis Carter and Thomas Gilovich, "The Relative Relativity of Material and Experiential Purchases," *Journal of Personality and Social*

Psychology 98, no. 1 (2010): 146–59.

28. Emily Rosenzweig and Thomas Gilovich, "Buyer's Remorse or Missed Opportunity? Differential Regrets for Material and Experiential Purchases," *Journal of Personality and Social Psychology* 102, no. 2 (February 2012): 215–23.
29. Carter and Gilovich, "The Relative Relativity of Material and Experiential Purchases," *Journal of Personality and Social Psychology* 98, no. 1 (2010): 146–59.
30. Rosenzweig and Gilovich, "Buyer's Remorse or Missed Opportunity? Differential Regrets for Material and Experiential Purchases," *Journal of Personality and Social Psychology* 102, no. 2 (February 2012): 215–23.
31. Carter and Gilovich, "The Relative Relativity of Material and Experiential Purchases."
32. Julian Villanueva, Luc Wathieu, and Michael I. Norton, "elBulli: The Taste of Innovation," *Harvard Business School Cases* (July 2008): 1.
33. http://chocolateandzucchini.com/archives/2006/08/dinner_at_el_bulli.php.
34. Ibid.
35. Barbara Frederickson and Daniel Kahneman, "Duration Neglect in Retrospective Evaluations of Affective Episodes," *Journal of Personality and Social Psychology* 65, no. 1 (1993): 45–55.
36. Simon Kemp, Christopher D. B. Burt, and Laura Furneaux, "A Test of the Peak-End Rule with Extended Autobiographical Events," *Memory & Cognition* 36, no. 1 (2008): 132–38.
37. Author interview with Laszlo Bock, March 20, 2012.
38. Nira Liberman and Yaacov Trope, "The Psychology of Transcending the Here and Now," *Science* 322, no. 5905 (November 2008): 1201–05.
39. Van Boven and Gilovich, "To Do or to Have? That Is the Question."
40. Ibid.

Chapter Two. Make It a Treat

1. Sarah Silverman, *The Bedwetter: Stories of Courage, Redemption, and Pee* (New York: HarperCollins, 2010).
2. Jordi Quoidbach and Elizabeth W. Dunn, "Give It Up: A Strategy for Combatting Hedonic Adaptation," *Social Psychological and Personality Science* 4, no. 5 (January 2013): 563–68.
3. Norbert Schwarz and Jing Xu, "Why Don't We Learn from Poor Choices? The Consistency of Expectations, Choice, and Memory Clouds the Lesson of Experience." *Journal of Consumer Psychology 21*, no. 2 (April 2011): 142–145.
4. Oprah Winfrey, "The Magic of Gratitude," *Oprah Radio*, 2008, http://www.oprah.com/oprahradio/The-Magic-of-Gratitude_1.

5. Sara B. Algoe, Jonathan Haidt, and Shelly L. Gable, "Beyond Reciprocity: Gratitude and Relationships in Everyday Life," *Emotion* 8, no. 3 (June 2008): 425–29; Minkyung Koo, Sara B. Algoe, Timothy D. Wilson, and Daniel T. Gilbert, "It's a Wonderful Life: Mentally Subtracting Positive Events Improves People's Affective States, Contrary to Their Affective Forecasts," *Journal of Personality and Social Psychology* 95, no. 5 (November 2008): 1217–24.
6. Jordi Quoidbach, Elizabeth W. Dunn, K. V. Petrides, and Moïra Mikolajczak, "Money Giveth, Money Taketh Away: The Dual Effect of Wealth on Happiness," *Psychological Science* 21, no. 6 (June 2010): 759–63.
7. Kathleen D. Vohs, Nicole L. Mead, and Miranda R. Goode, "The Psychological Consequences of Money," *Science* 314, no. 5802 (November 2006): 1154–56.
8. Quoidbach, Dunn, Petrides, and Mikolajczak, "Money Giveth, Money Taketh Away."
9. Roald Dahl, *Charlie and the Chocolate Factory* (London: Penguin Books, 1964), 8–9.
10. Quoidbach, Dunn, Petrides, and Mikolajczak, "Money Giveth, Money Taketh Away."
11. Silverman, *The Bedwetter*.
12. Jing Wang, Nathan Novemsky, and Ravi Dhar, "Anticipating Adaptation to Products," *Journal of Consumer Research* 36, no. 2 (August 2009): 149–59.
13. Ibid.
14. Shane Frederick and George Loewenstein, "Hedonic Adaptation," in *Well-being: The Foundations of Hedonic Psychology*, ed. Daniel Kahneman, Edward Diener, and Norbert Schwarz (New York: Russell Sage, 1999), 320.
15. Quoidbach and Dunn, "Give It Up."
16. The Great American Apparel Diet, http://www.thegreatamericanapPareldiet.com.
17. Six Items or Less, http://sixitemsorless.com.
18. Allison Glock, "Back to Basics: Living with 'Voluntary Simplicity,'" *O, The Oprah Magazine*, January 2009, http://www.oprah.com/omagazine/Meet-Followers-of-the-Simple-Living-Philosophy.
19. Kirk Warren Brown and Tim Kasser, "Are Psychological and Ecological Well-Being Compatible? The Role of Values, Mindfulness, and Lifestyle," *Social Indicators Research* 74, no. 2 (November 2005): 349–68.
20. Jaime L. Kurtz, "Looking to the Future to Appreciate the Present: The Benefits of Perceived Temporal Scarcity," *Psychological Science* 19, no. 12 (December 2008): 1238–41.
21. Laura L. Carstensen, Helene H. Fung, and Susan T. Charles, "Socioemotional Selectivity Theory and the Regulation of Emotion in the Second

Half of Life," *Motivation and Emotion* 27, no. 2 (June 2003): 103–23.
22. *Newsweek*, March 6, 1995.
23. Suzanne B. Shu and Ayelet Gneezy, "Procrastination of Enjoyable Experiences," *Journal of Marketing Research* 47, no. 5 (October 2010): 933–44.
24. "Euromonitor International's Top City Destinations Ranking," *Euromonitor International*, January 6, 2011, http://blog.euromonitor.com/2011/01/euromonitor-internationals-top-city-destinations-ranking.html.
25. Shu and Gneezy, "Procrastination of Enjoyable Experiences."
26. Fiscal 2006 Annual Report, Best Buy, http://library.corporateir.net/library/83-831-83192/items/199546/bby_ar06.pdf.
27. Author interview with David Vivenes, September 29, 2011.
28. "Canada Doubled Down–1 Million Sandwiches Sold," KFC Canada, November 15, 2010, http://www.marketwire.com/press-release/canada-doubled-down-1-million-sandwiches-sold-1353074.html.
29. Coca-Cola Company Heritage Timeline, http://heritage.coca-cola.com/timeline.swf.
30. Author interview with Ashlee Yingling, April 17, 2012.
31. "McRib Boosts McDonald's November Sales," MSNBC, December 8, 2010, http://www.msnbc.msn.com/id/40566036/ns/business-us_business.
32. Daniel Richards, "Walt Disney—A Look at the Man Behind Mickey Mouse," http://entrepreneurs.about.com/od/famousentrepreneurs/p/waltdisney.html.
33. Robert B. Cialdini, *Influence: Science and Practice*, 4th ed. (Boston: Pearson Education, 2001), 241.
34. Ibid., 266.
35. Author interview with Robin Chase, October 5, 2011.
36. Classic Car Club Manhattan, http://classiccarclubmanhattan.com.
37. Kate Hughes, "How to Live Like a Millionaire—Even If It's Only Part-Time," *Independent*, March 1, 2008, http://www.independent.co.uk/money/spend-save/how-to-live-like-a-millionaire-ndash-even-ifits-only-parttime-789840.html.
38. David Budworth, "Live It Up at a Fraction of the Cost," *Sunday Times*, August 5, 2007.
39. Leif D. Nelson, Tom Meyvis, and Jeff Galak, "Enhancing the Television-Viewing Experience through Commercial Interruptions," *Journal of Consumer Research* 36, no. 2 (August 2009): 160–72.
40. Leif D. Nelson and Tom Meyvis, "Interrupted Consumption: Disrupting Adaptation to Hedonic Experiences," *Journal of Marketing Research* 45, no. 6 (December 2008): 654–64.
41. Ibid.
42. Ibid.

43. Jordi Quoidbach, Elizabeth W. Dunn, Gaélle M. Bustin, and Cédric A. Bouquet, "The Price of Awesomeness: How a Wealth of Experiences Impoverishes Savoring" (forthcoming).
44. Ibid.
45. H. H. the Dalai Lama and Howard C. Cutler, *The Art of Happiness: A Handbook for Living* (New York: Riverhead Books, 1998); Oprah Winfrey, "The Magic of Gratitude," *Oprah Radio*, 2008, http://www.oprah.com/oprahradio/The-Magic-of-Gratitude_1.
46. Elizabeth W. Dunn, Jeremy C. Biesanz, Lauren J. Human, and Stephanie Finn, "Misunderstanding the Affective Consequences of Everyday Social Interactions: the Hidden Benefits of Putting One's Best Face Forward," *Journal of Personality and Social Psychology* 92, no. 6 (June 2007): 990–1005.
47. Arthur Aron, Christina C. Norman, Elaine N. Aron, Colin McKenna, and Richard E. Heyman, "Couples' Shared Participation in Novel and Arousing Activities and Experienced Relationship Quality," *Journal of Personality and Social Psychology* 78, no. 2 (2000): 273–84.
48. E. B. Hale and John O. Almquist, "Relation of Sexual Behavior to Germ Cell Output in Farm Animals," *Journal of Dairy Science* 43, supp. 1(1960): 145–67, cited in Timothy D. Wilson and Daniel T. Gilbert, "Explaining Away: A Model of Affective Adaptation," *Perspectives on Psychological Science* 3, no. 5 (September 2008): 376.
49. I. Tsapelas, A. Aron, and T. Orbuch, "Marital Boredom Now Predicts Less Satisfaction 9 Years Later," *Psychological Science* 20, no. 5 (May 2009): 543–45.
50. Charmin, http://www.charmin.com/en_us/pages/offers_ploza.shtml.
51. David T. Neal, Wendy Wood, Mengju Wu, and David Kurlander, "The Pull of the Past: When Do Habits Persist Despite Conflict With Motives?," *Personality & Social Psychology Bulletin* 37, no. 11 (November 2011): 1428–37.
52. Paul Rozin, "The Meaning of Food in Our Lives: A Cross-Cultural Perspective on Eating and Well-Being," *Journal of Nutrition Education & Behavior* 37 (November 2, 2005): S107–S112.
53. Ibid.
54. Paul Rozin, Kimberly Kabnick, Erin Pete, Claude Fischler, and Christy Shields, "The Ecology of Eating: Smaller Portion Sizes in France Than in the United States Help Explain the French Paradox," *Psychological Science* 14, no. 5 (September 2003): 450–54.
55. Ran Kivetz and Itamar Simonson, "Earning the Right to Indulge: Effort as a Determinant of Customer Preferences Toward Frequency Program Rewards," *Journal of Marketing Research* 39, no. 2 (May 2002): 155–70.
56. Jing Xu and Norbert Schwarz, "Do We Really Need a Reason to

Indulge?," *Journal of Marketing Research* 46, no. 1 (February 2009): 25–36.

57. Kivetz and Simonson, "Earning the Right to Indulge."
58. Christopher K. Hsee, "Value Seeking and Prediction–Decision Inconsistency: Why Don't People Take What They Predict They'll Like the Most?," *Psychonomic Bulletin & Review* 6, no. 4 (December 1999): 555–61.
59. Christopher K. Hsee, Jiao Zhang, Fang Yu, and Yiheng Xi, "Lay Rationalism and Inconsistency between Predicted Experience and Decision," *Journal of Behavioral Decision Making* 16, no. 4 (2003): 257–72.
60. Carey K. Morewedge, Daniel T. Gilbert, Boaz Keysar, Michael J. Berkovits, and Timothy D. Wilson, "Mispredicting the Hedonic Benefits of Segregated Gains," *Journal of Experimental Psychology: General* 136, no. 4 (2007): 700–709.

Chapter Three. Buy Time

1. The Onion, http://www.theonion.com/articles/national-news-highlights,25578/.
2. Daniel Kahneman, Alan B. Krueger, David Schkade, Norbert Schwarz, and Arthur A. Stone, "Would You Be Happier If You Were Richer? A Focusing Illusion," *Science* 312, no. 5782 (June 2006): 1908–10.
3. Ibid.
4. A. Krueger, D. Kahneman, C. Fischler, D. Schkade, N. Schwarz, and A. Stone, "Time Use and Subjective Well-Being in France and the U.S.," *Social Indicators Research* 93, no. 1 (2008): 7–18.
5. Nathan Zeldes, David Sward, and Sigal Louchheim, "Infomania: Why We Can't Afford to Ignore It Any Longer," *First Monday* 12, no. 8 (2007), http://firstmonday.org/htbin/cgiwrap/bin/ojs/index.php/fm/article/view/1973/1848.
6. Pico Iyer, "The Joy of Quiet," *New York Times*, December 29, 2011, http://www.nytimes.com/2012/01/01/opinion/sunday/the-joy-of-quiet.html.
7. Daniel Kahneman, Alan B. Krueger, David A. Schkade, Norbert Schwarz, and Arthur A. Stone, "A Survey Method for Characterizing Daily Life Experience: The Day Reconstruction Method," *Science* 306, no. 5702 (December 3, 2004): 1776–80.
8. Tim Kasser and Kennon M. Sheldon, "Time Affluence as a Path toward Personal Happiness and Ethical Business Practice: Empirical Evidence from Four Studies," *Journal of Business Ethics* 84, no. S2 (2008): 243–55.
9. Ronald J. Burke, Mustafa Koyuncu, Lisa Fiksenbaum, and Halil Demirer, "Time Affluence, Material Affluence and Well-Being among Turkish Managers," *Cross Cultural Management: An International Journal* 16, no. 4 (2009): 386–97.

10. Kasser and Sheldon, "Time Affluence as a Path toward Personal Happiness and Ethical Business Practice."
11. Ibid.
12. Matthew A. Killingsworth and Daniel T. Gilbert, "A Wandering Mind Is an Unhappy Mind," *Science* 330, no. 6006 (November 12, 2010): 932.
13. Kasser and Sheldon, "Time Affluence as a Path toward Personal Happiness and Ethical Business Practice."
14. Daniel S. Hamermesh and Jungmin Lee, "Stressed Out on Four Continents: Time Crunch or Yuppie Kvetch?," *Review of Economics & Statistics* 89, no. 2 (May 2007): 374–83.
15. Weiting Ng, Ed Diener, Raksha Aurora, and James Harter, "Affluence, Feelings of Stress, and Well-Being," *Social Indicators Research* 94, no. 2 (2008): 257–71.
16. John P. Robinson and Geoffrey Godbey, "Busyness as Usual," *Social Research* 72, no. 2 (Summer 2005): 407–26; Juliet B. Schor, "Working Hours and Time Pressure: The Controversy about Trends in Time Use," in *Working Time: International Trends, Theory and Policy Perspectives*, ed. Lonnie Golden and Deborah M. Figart, *Advances in Social Economics* (New York: Routledge, 2000), 73–86.
17. Ibid.
18. Mark Aguiar and Erik Hurst, "A Summary of Trends in American Time Allocation: 1965–2005," *Social Indicators Research* 93, no. 1 (2009): 57–64.
19. Sanford E. DeVoe and Jeffrey Pfeffer, "Time Is Tight: How Higher Economic Value of Time Increases Feelings of Time Pressure," *Journal of Applied Psychology* 96, no. 4 (July 2011): 665–76.
20. Ibid.
21. Allen D. Kanner, James C. Coyne, Catherine Schaefer, and Richard S. Lazarus, "Comparison of Two Modes of Stress Measurement: Daily Hassles and Uplifts Versus Major Life Events," *Journal of Behavioral Medicine* 4, no. 1 (1981): 1–39.
22. Susan Aschoff, "Salad Shooter," *Saint Petersburg Times*, September 23, 1999, http://www.sptimes.com/News/92399/Taste/Salad_shooter_shtml.
23. Chen-Bo Zhong and Sanford E. DeVoe, "You Are How You Eat: Fast Food and Impatience," *Psychological Science* 21, no. 5 (May 2010): 619–22.
24. Cassie Mogilner, Zoe Chance, and Michael I. Norton, "Giving Time Gives You Time," *Psychological Science* 23, no. 10 (October 2012): 1233–38.
25. Author interview with Paulette Minard, February 2, 2012.
26. Lee Boyce, "Pet inflation: How owning a cat or a dog will cost you £17k over its life," This is Money, September 28, 2011, http://www.

thisismoney.co.uk/money/bills/article-2042014/How-does-cost-dog-cat.html.
27. Tara Parker-Pope, "The Best Walking Partner: Man vs. Dog," *New York Times*, December 14, 2009, http://well.blogs.nytimes.com/2009/12/14/the-best-walking-partner-man-vs-dog.
28. Daniel Mochon, Michael I. Norton, and Dan Ariely, "Getting Off the Hedonic Treadmill, One Step at a Time: The Impact of Regular Religious Practice and Exercise on Well-Being," *Journal of Economic Psychology* 29, no. 5 (November 2008): 632–42.
29. Matthew B. Ruby, Elizabeth W. Dunn, Andrea Perrino, Randall Gillis, and Sasha Viel, "The Invisible Benefits of Exercise," *Health Psychology* 30, no. 1 (January 2011): 67–74.
30. E. K. Nisbet and J. M. Zelenski, "Underestimating Nearby Nature: Affective Forecasting Errors Obscure the Happy Path to Sustainability," *Psychological Science* 22, no. 9 (September 2011): 1101–6.
31. Krueger, Kahneman, Fischler, Schkade, Schwarz, and Stone, "Time Use and Subjective Well-Being in France and the U.S."
32. "Americans Now Spend over 100 Hours a Year Commuting," http://usgovinfo.about.com/od/censusandstatistics/a/commutetimes.htm.
33. Anita Elash, "Are We Reaching Peak Car?," *Globe & Mail*, October 22, 2011, http://www.theglobeandmail.com/news/national/are-we-reaching-peak-car/article2210139/.
34. Krueger, Kahneman, Fischler, Schkade, Schwarz, and Stone, "Time Use and Subjective Well-Being in France and the U.S."
35. Alois Stutzer and Bruno S. Frey, "Stress That Doesn't Pay: The Commuting Paradox," *Scandinavian Journal of Economics* 110, no. 2 (2008): 339–66. Unless cited otherwise, all statistics in this section are from Stutzer and Frey.
36. Ibid.
37. Author interview with Robin Chase, October 5, 2011.
38. James D. Schwartz, "Americans Work 2 Hours Each Day to Pay For Their Cars," *Urban Country Bicycle Blog*, May 6, 2011, http://www.theurbancountry.com/2011/05/americans-work-2-hours-each-day-to-pay.html.
39. Stutzer and Frey, "Stress That Doesn't Pay."
40. Richard E. Wener and Gary W. Evans, "Comparing Stress of Car and Train Commuters," *Transportation Research Part F: Traffic Psychology and Behaviour* 14, no. 2 (2011): 111–16.
41. "Telescope: A look at the nation's changing viewing habits from TV Licensing," TV Licensing, March 2012, http://www.tvlicensing.co.uk/resources/library/BBC/MEDIA_CENTRE/TV_Licensing_Telescope_Report_2012.pdf.
42. Giacomo Corneo, "Work and Television," *European Journal of Political*

Economy 21, no. 1 (2005): 99–113.

43. Alan B. Krueger, "Are We Having More Fun Yet? Categorizing and Evaluating Changes in Time Allocation," *Brookings Papers On Economic Activity* no. 2 (August 2007): 193–215; Krueger, Kahneman, Fischler, Schkade, Schwarz, and Stone, "Time Use and Subjective Well-Being in France and the U.S."; Killingsworth and Gilbert, "A Wandering Mind Is an Unhappy Mind."
44. Krueger, "Are We Having More Fun Yet?"
45. Bruno S. Frey, Christine Benesch, and Alois Stutzer, "Does Watching TV Make Us Happy?," *Journal of Economic Psychology* 28, no. 3 (June 2007): 283–313.
46. Kahneman, Krueger, Schkade, Schwarz, and Stone, "A Survey Method for Characterizing Daily Life Experience"; Krueger, "Are We Having More Fun Yet?"
47. Jennifer Senior, "Why Parents Hate Parenting." *New York*, July 4, 2010, http://nymag.com/news/features/67024/; Shankar Vedantam, "Parents Are Junkies," *Slate*, November 12, 2010, http://www.slate.com/articles/health_and_science/the_hidden_brain/2010/11/parents_are_junkies.html.
48. Krueger, "Are We Having More Fun Yet?" See also Katherine S. Nelson, Kostadin Kushlev, Tammy English, Elizabeth W. Dunn, and Sonja Lyubomirsky, "In Defense of Parenthood: Children Are Associated with More Joy than Misery," *Psychological Science 24*, no. 1 (January 2013): 3–10.
49. Ami Sedghi, "How much does it cost to raise a child in 2013 compared to a decade ago," *The Guardian*. January 24, 2013, http://www.guardian.co.uk/news/datablog/2013/jan/24/cost-to-raise-a-child-compared-to-decade-ago.
50. "Americans Eager to Take Back Their Time," http://205.153.117.210/about/polls/timepoll.php.
51. Krueger, Kahneman, Fischler, Schkade, Schwarz, and Stone, "Time Use and Subjective Well-Being in France and the U.S."
52. Daniel S. Hamermesh and Jungmin Lee, "Stressed Out on Four Continents: Time Crunch or Yuppie Kvetch?," *Review of Economics & Statistics* 89, no. 2 (May 2007): 374–83.
53. "Shannon Deegan: How Google's 20 Percent Time Fosters Innovation," http://www.youtube.com/watch?v=KwwdtQHqd9g.
54. "Google—Overview, Company Culture and History," http://jobsearchtech.about.com/od/companyprofiles/a/google.html.
55. Bai Kang and Michael T. Miller, "An Overview of the Sabbatical Leave in Higher Education: A Synopsis of the Literature Base," ERIC Document Reproductive Service No. ED 430 471 (1999).
56. Author interview with Elaine Mah (country manager, Intel of

Canada), January 13, 2012.

57. Steve Hamm, "A Passion for the Planet", *Bloomberg Businessweek*, August 21, 2006, http://www.businessweek.com/magazine/content/06_34/b3998431.htm.
58. Author interview with Elizabeth and Barbara Pagano, January 12, 2012.
59. G. Zauberman and J. G. Lynch Jr., "Resource Slack and Propensity to Discount Delayed Investments of Time Versus Money," *Journal of Experimental Psychology* 134, no. 1 (February 2005): 23–37.
60. Christopher K. Hsee and Jiao Zhang, "General Evaluability Theory," *Perspectives on Psychological Science* 5, no. 4 (November 2010): 343–55.
61. Richard A. Easterlin, "Explaining Happiness," *Proceedings of the National Academy of Sciences of the United States of America* 100, no. 19 (September 16, 2003): 11176–83.
62. Nira Liberman and Yaacov Trope, "The Psychology of Transcending the Here and Now," *Science* 322, no. 5905 (November 2008): 1201–1205.
63. Timothy D. Wilson, Thalia Wheatley, Jonathan M. Meyers, Daniel T. Gilbert, and Danny Axsom, "Focalism: A Source of Durability Bias in Affective Forecasting," *Journal of Personality and Social Psychology* 78, no. 5 (2000): 821–36.
64. Cassie Mogilner, "The Pursuit of Happiness: Time, Money, and Social Connection," *Psychological Science* 21, no. 9 (September 2010): 1348–54.
65. Cassie Mogilner and Jennifer Aaker, "'The Time vs. Money Effect': Shifting Product Attitudes and Decisions through Personal Connection," *Journal of Consumer Research* 36, no. 2 (2009): 277–91.
66. Mogilner, "The Pursuit of Happiness."
67. Ibid.
68. Wendy Liu and Jennifer Aaker, "The Happiness of Giving: The Time-Ask Effect," *Journal of Consumer Research* 35, no. 3 (2008): 543–57.
69. Mogilner and Aaker, "'The Time vs. Money Effect.'"
70. Ibid.
71. In A. C. Houston, ed., *Franklin: The Autobiography and Other Writings on Politics, Economics, and Virtue* (New York: Cambridge University Press, 2004).
72. Sanford E. DeVoe and Julian House, "Time, Money, and Happiness: How Does Putting a Price on Time Affect Our Ability to Smell the Roses?," *Journal of Experimental Social Psychology* 48, no. 2 (March 2012): 466–74.
73. Sanford E. DeVoe and Jeffrey Pfeffer, "When Time Is Money: The Effect of Hourly Payment on the Evaluation of Time," *Organizational Behavior and Human Decision Processes* 104, no. 1 (2007): 1–13.
74. Sanford E. DeVoe, Byron Y. Lee, and Jeffrey Pfeffer, "Hourly versus

Salaried Payment and Decisions about Trading Time and Money over Time," *Industrial and Labor Relations Review* 63, no. 4 (July 2010): 627–40.

75. DeVoe and Pfeffer, "When Time Is Money."
76. Ibid.

Chapter Four. Pay Now, Consume Later

1. Emily S. Gerson and Ben Woolsey, "The history of credit cards," May 2009, http://www.creditcards.com/credit-card-news/credit-cards-history-1264.php.
2. Consumer Electronics Association, "CEA Projects 'Digital Holiday Season' with Increased Spending on Electronics, Gifts Overall," press release, 2010, http://www.businesswire.com/news/home/20111025006661/en/CEA-Projects-%E2%80%98Digital-Holiday-Season%E2%80%99-Increased-Spending.
3. Jeroen Nawijn, Miquelle A. Marchand, Ruut Veenhoven, and Ad J. Vingerhoets, "Vacationers Happier, But Most Not Happier After a Holiday," *Applied Research in Quality of Life* 5, no. 1 (March 2010): 35–47.
4. Julia A. Weiler, Boris Suchan, and Irene Daum, "When the Future Becomes the Past: Differences in Brain Activation Patterns for Episodic Memory and Episodic Future Thinking," *Behavioural Brain Research* (April 2010).
5. Eugene M. Caruso, Daniel T. Gilbert, and Timothy D. Wilson, "A Wrinkle in Time: Asymmetric Valuation of Past and Future Events," *Psychological Science* 19, no. 8 (August 2008): 796–801.
6. Michael A. Andrykowski and William H. Redd, "Longitudinal Analysis of the Development of Anticipatory Nausea," *Journal of Consulting and Clinical Psychology* 55, no. 1 (February 1987): 36–41.
7. Peter Sheridan Dodds and Christopher M. Danforth, "Measuring the Happiness of Large-Scale Written Expression: Songs, Blogs, and Presidents," *Journal of Happiness Studies* 11, no. 4 (August 2010): 441–56.
8. Scott A. Golder and Michael W. Macy, "Diurnal and Season Mood Vary with Work, Sleep, and Daylength across Diverse Cultures," *Science* 333, no. 6051 (September 2011): 1878–81.
9. Maurice L. Farber, "Time-Perspective and Feeling-Tone: A Study in The Perception of the Days," *Journal of Psychology: Interdisciplinary and Applied* 35 (1953): 256.
10. Matthew A. Killingsworth and Daniel T Gilbert, "A Wandering Mind Is an Unhappy Mind," *Science* 330, no. 6006 (November 12, 2010): 932.
11. Andrew K. MacLeod, B. Pankhania, M. Lee, and D. Mitchell, "Parasuicide, Depression and the Anticipation of Positive and Negative Future

Experiences," *Psychological Medicine: A Journal of Research in Psychiatry and the Allied Sciences* 27, no. 4 (July 1997): 973–77. For a brief review of this area of research, see Jordi Quoidbach, Alex M. Wood, and Michel Hansenne, "Back to the Future: The Effect of Daily Practice of Mental Time Travel into the Future on Happiness and Anxiety," *Journal of Positive Psychology* 4, no. 5 (September 2009): 349–55.

12. Roger Buehler, Cathy McFarland, Vassili Spyropoulos, and Kent C. H. Lam, "Motivated Prediction of Future Feelings: Effects of Negative Mood and Mood Orientation on Affective Forecasts," *Personality and Social Psychology Bulletin* 33, no. 9 (September 2007): 1265–78.
13. Brian Knutson and Richard Peterson, "Neurally Reconstructing Expected Utility," *Games and Economic Behavior* 52, no. 2 (August 2005): 305–15.
14. Quoidbach, Wood, and Hansenne, "Back to the Future."
15. Author interview with Marcia Fiamengo, August 4, 2011.
16. Author interview with Barbara Messing, November 14, 2011.
17. Michael I. Norton, Jeana H. Frost, and Dan Ariely, "Less Is More: The Lure of Ambiguity, or Why Familiarity Breeds Contempt," *Journal of Personality and Social Psychology* 92, no. 1 (January 2007): 97–105.
18. David Remnick, "The Masochism Campaign: Say Anything about Tony Blair, He Can Take It," *New Yorker*, May 2, 2005, http://archives.newyorker.com/?i=2005-05-02#folio=074.
19. United States presidential approval rating, http://en.wikipedia.org/wiki/United_States_presidential_approval_rating.
20. Jaime L. Kurtz, Timothy D. Wilson, and Daniel T. Gilbert, "Quantity versus Uncertainty: When Winning One Prize Is Better Than Winning Two," *Journal of Experimental Social Psychology* 43, no. 6 (November 2007): 979–85.
21. Author interview with Katia Beauchamp and Hayley Barna, October 5, 2011.
22. Knutson and Peterson, "Neurally Reconstructing Expected Utility."
23. For a thorough discussion of this issue, see Roy F. Baumeister, Kathleen D. Vohs, C. Nathan DeWall, and Liqing Zhang, "How Emotion Shapes Behavior: Feedback, Anticipation, and Reflection, Rather Than Direct Causation," *Personality and Social Psychology Review* 11, no. 2 (2007): 167–203.
24. Timothy D. Wilson, Douglas J. Lisle, Dolores Kraft, and Christopher G. Wetzel, "Preferences As Expectation-Driven Inferences: Effects of Affective Expectations on Affective Experience," *Journal of Personality and Social Psychology* 56, no. 4 (April 1989): 519–30.
25. Michael I. Norton and George R. Goethals, "Spin (and Pitch) Doctors: Campaign Strategies in Televised Political Debates," *Political Behavior* 26, no. 3 (September 2004): 227–48.
26. "National Travel Survey", Department for Transport Statistics, 2011.

27. Stephen M. Nowlis, Naomi Mandel, and Deborah Brown McCabe, "The Effect of a Delay between Choice and Consumption on Consumption Enjoyment," *Journal of Consumer Research* 31, no. 3 (December 2004): 502–10.
28. Ibid.
29. Karim S. Kassam, Daniel T. Gilbert, Andrew Boston, and Timothy D. Wilson, "Future Anhedonia and Time Discounting," *Journal of Experimental Social Psychology* 44, no. 6 (November 2008): 1533–37.
30. On Amir and Dan Ariely, "Decisions by Rules: The Case of Unwillingness to Pay for Beneficial Delays," *Journal of Marketing Research* 44, no. 1 (February 2007): 142–52.
31. George Loewenstein, "Anticipation and the Value of Delayed Consumption," *Economic Journal* 97, no. 387 (September 1987): 666–84.
32. Ryan W. Buell and Michael I. Norton, "The Labor Illusion: How Operational Transparency Increases Perceived Value," *Marketing Science* 57, no. 9 (September 2011): 1564–79.
33. Drazen Prelec and George Loewenstein, "The Red and the Black: Mental Accounting of Savings and Debt," *Marketing Science* 17, no. 1 (March 1998): 4.
34. Xinyue Zhou, Kathleen D. Vohs, and Roy F. Baumeister, "The Symbolic Power of Money: Reminders of Money Alter Social Distress and Physical Pain," *Psychological Science* 20, no. 6 (June 2009): 700–706.
35. Brian Knutson, Scott Rick, G. Elliott Wimmer, Drazen Prelec, and George Loewenstein, "Neural Predictors of Purchases," *Neuron* 53, no. 1 (January 4, 2007): 147–56.
36. "The Invention of Money," *This American Life*, National Public Radio, January 7, 2011, http://www.thisamericanlife.org/radio-archives/episode/423/the-invention-of-money.
37. The Onion, "Visa Exposed as Massive Credit Card Scam," August 15, 2011, http://www.theonion.com/articles/visa-exposed-as-massive-credit-card-scam,21136.
38. Drazen Prelec and Duncan Simester, "Always Leave Home Without It: A Further Investigation of the Credit-Card Effect on Willingness to Pay," *Marketing Letters* 12, no. 1 (February 2001): 5–12.
39. Dilip Soman, "Effects of Payment Mechanism on Spending Behavior: The Role of Rehearsal and Immediacy of Payments," *Journal of Consumer Research* 27, no. 4 (March 2001): 460–74.
40. Kimberly Amadeo, "Average Credit Card Debt Still More than $6500 per Family," *About.com*, April 7, 2011, http://useconomy.about.com/b/2011/04/07/average-credit-card-debt-still-more-than-6500-per-family.htm. Statistic based on U.S. Census 2010, "Households and Families," http://www.census.gov/newsroom/releases/archives/families_households/cb10-174.html; Federal Reserve Statistical Release,

"Consumer Credit," April 6, 2012, http://www.federalreserve.gov/releases/g19/Current/.

41. Associated Press–GfK Poll, Roper Public Affairs & Media, 2010.
42. Ibid.
43. Wendy Johnson and Robert F. Krueger, "How Money Buys Happiness: Genetic and Environmental Processes Linking Finances and Life Satisfaction," *Journal of Personality and Social Psychology* 90, no. 4 (April 2006): 680–91.
44. Sarah Brown, Karl Taylor, and Stephen Wheatley Price, "Debt and Distress: Evaluating the Psychological Cost of Credit," *Journal of Economic Psychology* 26, no. 5 (October 2005): 642–63.
45. Jeffrey Dew, "Two Sides of the Same Coin? The Differing Roles of Assets and Consumer Debt in Marriage," *Journal of Family and Economic Issues* 28, no. 1 (March 2007): 89–104.
46. David J. Hardisty, Shane Frederick, and Elke U. Weber, "Dread Looms Larger than Pleasurable Anticipation," November 1, 2011, available at http://ssrn.com/abstract=1961370 or http://dx.doi.org/10.2139/ssrn.1961370.
47. Brown, Taylor, and Price, "Debt and Distress."
48. "Get Ready for the Pain of Paying," *Daily Beast*, August 29, 2008, http://www.thedailybeast.com/newsweek/2008/08/30/get-ready-for-the-pain-of-paying.html.
49. "Debit Card Use Remains Robust in Midst of Economic Downturn," PULSE 2010 Debt Issuer Study, https://www.pulsenetwork.com/public/about/pulse-news/press-releases/2010/debit-use.html.
50. Daljit Deshi, "Debit Card Usage Set to Surge in Malaysia," Asia News Network, April 18, 2011, http://ph.news.yahoo.com/debit-card-usage-set-surge-malaysia-20110417-224001-457.html.
51. Lee Jinkook, Fahzy Abdul-Rahman, and Kim Hyungsoo, "Debit Card Usage: An Examination of Its Impact on Household Debt," *Financial Services Review* 16, no. 1 (Spring 2007): 73–87.
52. Farhad Manjoo, "The End of the Credit Card? A New App Called Card Case Foretells a World Without Cash and Plastic." *Slate*, November 2, 2011, http://www.slate.com/articles/technology/technology/2011/11/card_case_the_new_payments_app_that_could_make_cash_and_plastic_.html.
53. Leaf Van Boven and Thomas Gilovich, "To Do or to Have? That Is the Question," *Journal of Personality and Social Psychology* 85, no. 6 (December 2003): 1193–1202.
54. Manoj Thomas, Kalpesh Kaushik Desai, and Satheeshkumar Seenivasan, "How Credit Card Payments Increase Unhealthy Food Purchases: Visceral Regulation of Vices," *Journal of Consumer Research* 38, no. 1 (June 2011): 126–39.

55. Katherine L. Milkman, Todd Rogers, and Max H. Bazerman, "I'll Have the Ice Cream Soon and the Vegetables Later: A Study of Online Grocery Purchases and Order Lead Time," *Marketing Letters* 21, no. 1 (March 2010): 17–35.
56. Ran Kivetz and Itamar Simonson, "Self-Control for the Righteous: Toward a Theory of Precommitment to Indulgence," *Journal of Consumer Research* 29, no. 2 (September 2002): 207.
57. Ibid., 209.
58. For a review see Nira Liberman and Yaacov Trope, "The Psychology of Transcending the Here and Now," *Science* 322, no. 5905 (November 2008): 1201–1205.
59. John T. Gourville and Dilip Soman, "Payment Depreciation: The Behavioral Effects of Temporally Separating Payments from Consumption," *Journal of Consumer Research* 25, no. 2 (September 1998): 160–74.

Chapter Five. Invest in Others

1. Warren Buffett, "My Philanthropic Pledge," *CNNMoney*, June 16, 2010, http://money.cnn.com/2010/06/15/news/newsmakers/Warren_Buffett_Pledge_Letter.fortune/index.html.
2. Elizabeth W. Dunn, Lara B. Aknin, and Michael I. Norton, "Spending Money on Others Promotes Happiness," *Science* 319, no. 5870 (March 2008): 1687–88.
3. Ibid.
4. Buffett, "My Philanthropic Pledge."
5. Lara B. Aknin et al., "Prosocial Spending and Well-Being: Cross-Cultural Evidence for a Psychological Universal," *Journal of Personality and Social Psychology 104*, no. 4 (April 2013): 635–52.
6. Ibid.
7. Lara B. Aknin, Kiley J. Hamlin, and Elizabeth W. Dunn, "Giving Leads to Happiness in Young Children," *Plos ONE* 7, no. 6 (June 2012).
8. Zosia Bielski, "Canvassers Take the Cause to the Street," *Globe & Mail*, November 1, 2011, http://www.theglobeandmail.com/life/giving/how-to-give/canvassers-take-the-cause-to-the-street/article2221151/page2/.
9. Netta Weinstein and Richard M. Ryan, "When Helping Helps: Autonomous Motivation for Prosocial Behavior and Its Influence on Well-Being for the Helper and Recipient," *Journal of Personality and Social Psychology* 98, no. 2 (February 2010): 222–44.
10. William T. Harbaugh, Ulrich Mayr, and Daniel R. Burghart, "Neural Responses to Taxation and Voluntary Giving Reveal Motives for Charitable Donations," *Science* 316, no. 5831 (June 2007): 1622–25.
11. "Giving & Volunteering in the United States," Independent Sector 2001, http://www.cpanda.org/pdfs/gv/GV01Report.pdf.

12. Weinstein and Ryan, "When Helping Helps."
13. "Euromillions £101m Jackpot Won by Cambridgeshire Couple," BBC News, October 11, 2011, http://www.bbc.co.uk/news/uk-england-15253038.
14. Esther Addley, "Euromillions Couple Gives Friends £1M Each," *Guardian*, October 11, 2011, http://www.guardian.co.uk/uk/2011/oct/11/euromillions-couple-give-friends-million-each.
15. "Euromillions £101m Jackpot Won by Cambridgeshire Couple."
16. Lydia Saad, "Americans Plan to Spend Same on Christmas 2011 as in 2010," *Gallup Poll Briefing* (October 20, 2011): 1, http://www.gallup.com/poll/150203/Americans-Plan-Spend-Christmas-2011-2010.aspx.
17. "Consumers to Take Conservative Approach to Holiday Shopping," National Retail Federation/BIG Research 2007, http://www.nrf.com/modules.php?name=news&op=viewlive&sp_id=386.
18. Joel Waldfogel, "The Deadweight Loss of Christmas," *American Economic Review* 83, no. 5 (December 1993): 1328–36, http://graphics8.nytimes.com/images/blogs/freakonomics/pdf/WaldfogelDeadweightLossXmas.pdf.
19. Elizabeth W. Dunn, Jeff Huntsinger, Janetta Lun, and Stacey Sinclair, "The Gift of Similarity: How Good and Bad Gifts Influence Relationships," *Social Cognition* 26, no. 4 (August 2008): 469–81.
20. Lara B. Aknin, Gillian M. Sandstrom, Elizabeth W. Dunn, and Michael I. Norton, "It's the Recipient That Counts: Spending Money on Strong Social Ties Leads to Greater Happiness Than Spending on Weak Social Ties," *Plos ONE* 6, no. 2 (February 2011).
21. Lara B. Aknin, Elizabeth W. Dunn, Gillian M. Sandstrom, and Michael I. Norton, "Turning Good Deeds into Good Feelings: The Value of the 'Social' in Prosocial Spending," unpublished data, University of British Columbia, 2012.
22. Ibid.
23. Author interview with Charles Best, March 18, 2012.
24. "Kevin Starr: Lasting Impact," http://poptech.org/popcasts/kevin_starr_lasting_impact.
25. Author interview with Kevin Starr, April 4, 2012.
26. Spread the Net, http://www.spreadthenet.org/.
27. Aknin, Lara. B., Elizabeth W. Dunn, Adam M. Grant, Ashley V. Whillans, and Michael I. Norton, "Feeling Like You Made a Difference: On the Importance of Perceived Prosocial Impact When Giving to Others," unpublished data, University of British Columbia, 2012.
28. Adam M. Grant and Sabine Sonnentag, "Doing Good Buffers against Feeling Bad: Prosocial Impact Compensates for Negative Task and Self-Evaluations," *Organizational Behavior and Human Decision*

Processes 111, no. 1 (January 2010): 13–22.
29. Author interview with Kevin Starr, March 28, 2012.
30. Lara B. Aknin, Elizabeth W. Dunn, and Michael I. Norton, "Happiness Runs in a Circular Motion: Evidence for a Positive Feedback Loop between Prosocial Spending and Happiness," *Journal of Happiness Studies* 13, no. 2 (April 2012): 347–55.
31. Dollar Collective, http://dollarcollective.wordpress.com.
32. Doerthe Keilholz, "Flashmob Meets Charity in New Collective," *openfile*, Vancouver, BC, February 29, 2012, http://vancouver.openfile.ca/vancouver/text/flashmob-meets-charity-new-collective.
33. William Michael Brown, Nathan S. Consedine, and Carol Magai, "Altruism Relates to Health in an Ethnically Diverse Sample of Older Adults," *Journals of Gerontology: Series B: Psychological Sciences and Social Sciences* 60B, no. 3 (May 2005): P143–P152.
34. Elizabeth W. Dunn, Claire E. Ashton-James, Margaret D. Hanson, and Lara B. Aknin, "On the Costs of Self-Interested Economic Behavior: How Does Stinginess Get under the Skin?," *Journal of Health Psychology* 15, no. 4 (May 2010): 627–33.
35. Brian R, Walker, "Glucocorticoids and Cardiovascular Disease," *European Journal of Endocrinology* 157, no. 5 (November 2007): 545–59.
36. Zoë Chance and Michael I. Norton, "I Give, Therefore I Have: Giving and Subjective Wealth," working paper, Yale University.
37. Michael I. Norton and Jill J. Avery, *The Pepsi Refresh Project: A Thirst for Change*, Harvard Business School Case 512-018.
38. Ibid.
39. Lalin Anik, Lara B. Aknin, Michael I. Norton, Elizabeth W. Dunn, and Jordi Quiodbach, "Prosocial Bonuses Increase Employee Satisfaction and Team Performance," unpublished manuscript, Harvard University, 2012.
40. Author interview with Laszlo Bock, March 20, 2012.
41. Anik et al., "Prosocial Bonuses Increase Employee Satisfaction and Team Performance."
42. Ibid.
43. Michael I. Norton, Fiona Wilson, Jill J. Avery, and Thomas J. Steenburgh, *Better World Books*, Harvard Business School Case 511-057.
44. Ibid.
45. Aradhna Krishna, "Can Supporting a Cause Decrease Donations and Happiness? The Cause Marketing Paradox," *Journal of Consumer Psychology* 21, no. 3 (July 2011): 338–45.
46. Ibid.
47. Elizabeth W. Dunn, Lara B. Aknin, and Michael I. Norton, "Spending Money on Others Promotes Happiness," *Science* 319, no. 5870 (March 2008): 1687–88.

48. Margery A. Beck, "Anonymous Donors Pay Off Kmart Layaway Accounts," Associated Press, December 16, 2011, http://sg.news.yahoo.com/anonymous-donors-pay-off-kmart-layaway-accounts-221000605.html.

Epilogue. Zooming Out

1. Wendy Johnson and Robert F. Krueger, "How Money Buys Happiness: Genetic and Environmental Processes Linking Finances and Life Satisfaction," *Journal of Personality and Social Psychology* 90, no. 4 (2006): 680–91.
2. Johanna Peetz and Roger Buehler, "Is There a Budget Fallacy? The Role of Savings Goals in the Prediction of Personal Spending," *Personality and Social Psychology Bulletin* 35, no. 12 (December 2009): 1579–91.
3. Gross National Happiness, http://www.grossnationalhappiness.com/.
4. David G. Myers, "Rules of Engagement," symposium talk, Langara College, Vancouver, BC, February 9, 2012.
5. Edward N. Wolff, "Recent Trends in Household Wealth in the United States: Rising Debt and the Middle-Class Squeeze—an Update 2007," Levy Economics Institute Working Paper, No. 589 (March 2010): 1–58, http://www.levyinstitute.org/pubs/wp_589.pdf.
6. Michael I. Norton and Dan Ariely, "Building a Better America–One Wealth Quintile at a Time," *Perspectives on Psychological Science* 6, no. 1 (January 2011): 9–12.
7. Shigehiro Oishi, Selin Kesebir, and Ed Diener, "Income Inequality and Happiness," *Psychological Science* 22, no. 9 (September 2011): 1095–1100.
8. Adam Seth Levine, Robert H. Frank, and Oege Dijk, "Expenditure Cascades," September 13, 2010, http://papers.ssrn.com/sol3/papers.cfm?abstract_id=1690612.
9. Rafael Di Tella, Robert J. MacCulloch, and Andrew J. Oswald, "The Macroeconomics of Happiness," *Review of Economics & Statistics* 85, no. 4 (November 2003): 809–27.
10. Richard A. Easterlin, "Does Economic Growth Improve the Human Lot? Some Empirical Evidence," in *Nations and Households in Economic Growth: Essays in Honour of Moses Abramovitz*, ed. P. A. David and M. W. Reder (New York and London: Academic Press: 1974); Richard A. Easterlin, "Will Raising the Incomes of All Increase the Happiness of All?," *Journal of Economic Behavior and Organization* 27, no. 1 (June 1995): 35–47; Richard A. Easterlin, Laura Angelescu McVey, Malgorzata Switek, Onnicha Sawangfa, and Jacqueline Smith Zweig, "The Happiness-Income Paradox Revisited," *Proceedings of the National Academy of Sciences of the United States of America* 107, no. 52 (December 28, 2010): 22463–68; Betsey Stevenson and Justin Wolfers, "Economic

Growth and Subjective Well-Being: Reassessing the Easterlin Paradox," Brookings Papers on Economic Activity, no. 1 (March 2008): 1–87.

11. Stevenson and Wolfers, "Economic Growth and Subjective Well-Being."
12. Alan B. Krueger, comment on Stevenson, Betsey, and Justin Wolfers, "Economic Growth and Subjective Well-Being: Reassessing the Easterlin Paradox." Brookings Papers on Economic Activity, no. 1 (March 2008): 1–87.
13. David Streitfeld and Megan Thee-Brenan, "Despite Fears, Owning Home Retains Allure, Poll Shows," *New York Times*, June 29, 2011, http://www.nytimes.com/2011/06/30/business/30poll.html.
14. Alex J. Pollock, "Why Canada Avoided a Mortgage Meltdown," *Wall Street Journal*, March 19, 2012, http://www.aei.org/article/economics/financial-services/why-canada-avoided-a-mortgage-meltdown.
15. "Somerville, MA: A Report on Well-being," http://www.somervillema.gov/sites/default/files/documents/Somerville_Well_Being_Report.pdf.
16. Soren Nyegaard, "Working Time in Denmark and US," LabourNet, http://www.labournet.net/docks2/0201/worktim1.htm.
17. "Which Country Gets the Most Vacation Days," CNBC, October 22, 2009, http://www.cnbc.com/id/33431347/Which_Country_Gets_the_Most_Vacation_Days.
18. Author interview with David Halpern, March 26, 2012.
19. Michael A. Tynan, Gabbi R. Promoff, and Allison MacNeil, "State Excise Taxes—United States, 2010–2011," Centers for Disease Control and Prevention, March 30, 2012, http://www.cdc.gov/mmwr/preview/mmwrhtml/mm6112a1.htm.
20. Lydia Saad, "Adult Smoking Ranges From 13% to 31% Across U.S. States," Gallup Well-Being Poll, August 26, 2010, http://www.gallup.com/poll/142694/adult-smoking-ranges-across-states.aspx.
21. Kathy McCabe, "Malden Restaurants Seek 10am Sunday Liquor Sales," *Boston Globe*, September 16, 2011, http://www.boston.com/yourtown/news/malden/2011/09/malden_restaurants_want_10_am.html.
22. Arkansas House Bill 1583 (Act 1220).
23. Jennifer Van Hook and Claire E. Altman, "Competitive Food Sales in Schools and Childhood Obesity: A Longitudinal Study," *Sociology of Education* 85, no. 1 (January 1, 2012): 23–39.
24. "How's Life? Measuring Well-Being," OECD Publishing, October 12, 2011, http://dx.doi.org/10.1787/9789264121164-en.
25. "OP Releases Request for Applications for a Live Near Your Work Pilot Program," Office of Planning, District of Columbia, April 29, 2011, http://planning.dc.gov/DC/Planning/About+Planning/News+Room/Press+Releases/OP+Releases+Request+for+Applicati

ons+for+a+Live+Near+Your+Work+Pilot+Program.

26. "Bicycling, Moving America Forward," Bikes Belong Coalition, 2008, http://www.bikesbelong.org/assets/documents/uploads/Bicycling_Booklet_08.pdf.
27. David R. Bassett, John Pucher Jr., Ralph Buehler, Dixie L. Thompson, and Scott E. Crouter, "Walking, Cycling, and Obesity Rates in Europe, North America, and Australia," *Journal of Physical Activity and Health*, no. 5 (2008): 795–814, http://policy.rutgers.edu/faculty/pucher/jpah08.pdf.
28. Richard Florida, "Bicycling and the Wealth and Happiness of Cities," Creative Class Group, June 27, 2011, http://www.creativeclass.com/_v3/creative_class/2011/06/27/bicycling-and-the-wealth-and-happiness-of-cities.
29. "The Nation's Top Taxman Shares His Workout Playlist," National Public Radio, April 16, 2012, http://www.npr.org/2012/04/16/150640347/the-nations-top-taxman-shares-his-workout-playlist.
30. "Know Before You Owe," Consumer Financial Protection Bureau, http://www.consumerfinance.gov/knowbeforeyouowe.
31. Warren Buffett, "Stop Coddling the Super-Rich," *New York Times*, August 14, 2011, http://www.nytimes.com/2011/08/15/opinion/stop-coddling-the-super-rich.html.
32. Daniel Politi, "Obama Pushes Lawmakers to Pass 'Buffett Rule' Tax," *Slate*, March 31, 2012, http://slatest.slate.com/posts/2012/03/31/buffett_rule_tax_obama_pushes_millionaire_tax_legislation.html.
33. Zak Maymin, "I Hate Income Tax: Seven Reasons to Remove the Greatest Evil Facing Americans," *Publicani*, August 4, 2011, http://www.publicani.com/i-hate-income-tax/.
34. "I Hate Taxes," http://www.facebook.com/NoTaxes.
35. Shigehiro Oishi, Ulrich Schimmack, and Ed Diener, "Progressive Taxation and the Subjective Well-Being of Nations," *Psychological Science* 23, no. 1 (January 2012): 86–92.
36. Harbaugh, Mayr, and Burghart, "Neural Responses to Taxation and Voluntary Giving Reveal Motives for Charitable Donations."
37. Cait P. Lamberton, "A Spoonful of Choice: How Allocation Increases Satisfaction with Tax Payments," *Journal of Public Policy and Marketing* (forthcoming).
38. "Part I. Taxation of Wage Income 2010," http://www.oecd.org/dataoecd/44/44/38402588.pdf.
39. "World Giving Index 2011: A Global View of Giving Trends," Charities Aid Foundation, https://www.cafonline.org/pdf/World_Giving_Index_2011_191211.pdf.
40. Scott Standley and David Roodman, "Tax Policies to Promote Private Charitable Giving in DAC Countries," Center for Global Development, Working Paper No. 82 (January 2006), http://ssrn.com/ab

stract=984021.

41. Bruno S. Frey and Alois Stutzer, *Happiness and Economics: How the Economy and Institutions Affect Human Well-being* (Princeton, NJ: Princeton University Press, 2002); Ronald Inglehart, *Culture Shift in Advanced Industrial Society* (Princeton, NJ: Princeton University Press, 1990).
42. John Helliwell, Richard Layard, and Jeffrey Sachs, "World Happiness Report," http://www.earth.columbia.edu/sitefiles/file/Sachs%20Writing/2012/World%20Happiness%20Report.pdf.
43. Xeni Jardin, "China's Internet Censors not Happy about UNs World Happiness Report," *BoingBoing*, Monday April 9, http://boingboing.net/2012/04/09/chinas-internet-censors-not.html.
44. The Onion, "Grown Adult Actually Expects to Be Happy," March 10, 2011, http://www.theonion.com/articles/grown-adult-actually-expects-to-be-happy.
45. Jonathan W. Schooler, Dan Ariely, and George Loewenstein, "The Pursuit and Assessment of Happiness May Be Self-Defeating," in *The Psychology of Economic Decisions*, ed. Juan D. Carrillo and Isabelle Brocas (Oxford: Oxford University Press, 2003), 41–70

Acknowledgments

Our research shows that helping others makes people happy, so we can only surmise that this book has provided a lot of happiness because, man, did we get a lot of help. From the very beginning, we received invaluable advice and encouragement from Dan Ariely, Chris Chabris, Dan Gilbert, Michael Gill, Jon Haidt, Sonja Lyubomirsky, Lauren Santucci, Jess Tracy, Bridget Wagner, and Tim Wilson, and our agent Katinka Matson and her team at the Brockman Agency.

The best part of writing this book was talking to so many interesting, funny, and smart people who shared their personal and professional stories of happy money with us, helping to bring our five principles to life. In particular, we thank Ferran Adrià (of elBulli), Deb Baldarelli, Hayley Barna and Katia Beauchamp (of Birchbox), Charles Best (of DonorsChoose.org), Laszlo Bock (of Google), Dan Brand, Travis Carter, Robin Chase (founder of Zipcar), Will Dean (of Tough Mudder), Marcia Fiamengo, Kiley Hamlin, David Halpern (of the Behavioural Insights Team), Ana Maria Irazabal (of Pepsi), Derek Lee, Elaine Mah (of Intel), Barbara Messing (of TripAdvisor), Paulette Minard (of Home Depot), Lisa and David Mogolov, David Murphy (of Better World Books), Elizabeth and Barbara Pagano (of yourSABBATICAL.com), Kevin Starr (of the Mulago Foundation), David Vivenes (of KFC), and the members of 2011 Duck Conference on Social Cognition (especially Elizabeth Haines, Cami Johnson, Steve Stroessner, and Amy Summerville).

We appreciate the incredible patience and wisdom of our wonderful editor Ben Loehnen, who taught us to resist the lure of long sentences, the passive voice, and—most especially—overuse of dashes. We were lucky to work with the great team at Simon & Schuster, particularly Jessica Abell and Kate Gales. We thank our research assistant Ashley Whillans, who spent many, many hours hunting down the people, facts, and findings we wanted to include in this book. Harvard Business School, the University of British Columbia, and the Social Sciences Research Council of Canada (SSHRC) all provided us with funding and support for this work.

We are forever grateful to the many friends and colleagues who read chapters of this book for us and tactfully pointed out places where readers might be misled, confused, offended, or otherwise made unhappy. Thanks to Jennifer Aaker, Lara Aknin, Lalin Anik, Robert Biswas-Diener, Travis Carter, Eugene Caruso, Zoë Chance, Alyssa Croft, Jan-Emmanuel De Neve, Sanford DeVoe, Ed Diener, Rafael Di Tella, Paul Dolan, Dan Gilbert, Tom Gilovich, John Gourville, Kiley Hamlin, John Helliwell, Ryan Howell, Uma Karmarkar, Jaime Kurtz, Kosta Kushlev, Cait Lamberton, Kristin Laurin, Kristi Lemm, Cassie Mogilner, Leif Nelson, Andrew Oswald, Jordi Quoidbach, Julio Rotemberg, Matt Ruby, Gillian Sandstrom, Rusty Silverstein, Leaf Van Boven, Kathleen Vohs, Ashley Whillans, and Tim Wilson, and special thanks to Mandy Catron. Although they may not agree with everything we say, they helped us say it better.

Finally, we want to thank our amazing graduate students

without whom most of our research that we discuss in this book wouldn't have happened: Lalin Anik, Ryan Buell, Zoë Chance, Lauren Human, Jordi Quoidbach, Matt Ruby, Gillian Sandstrom, and especially Lara Aknin, who was with us from the beginning in trying to show that sometimes, just sometimes, spending your money on other people makes you happy.

Index

abundance:
  as enemy of appreciation, xvi, 27–28, 37
  as sought by young people, 36
  see also treats
adaptation, 2, 34
  commercials and, 42–43, 44
Adrià, Ferran, xii, 18
advertising, 75–76, 126
Agriculture Department, U.S., 68
Aknin, Lara, 107–8, 110, 119
Alberta, University of, 131, 132
alcohol, 6, 146–47
American Cancer Society, 130
American Express, 79
anticipation, 82, 83–86, 87–89, 91, 93, 99
  see also delayed consumption
apparel, 136
Apple, 102
approval ratings, of presidents, 84
apps, 98
Arctic Ocean, 14, 15
Arkansas, 147
Arnhold, Rainer, 121
art, 6
art class, 67
artifical "mating" devices, 48
Ashlund, Stacey, 76
Australia, 45, 148

babysitters, 96
Baldarelli, Deb, 80
Bali, 45
Barna, Hayley, 85, 97
Beauchamp, Katia, 85, 97
behavioral economics, 92
Behavioural Insights Team, 139, 145–46
Belgium, xii, 31, 82, 128
Benjamin, 46–47
  sharing disdained by, 115
Benjamin Effect, 46–47
Best, Charles, 119–20
Best Buy, 38
Better World Books, 129–30
Beverly Hills, Calif., 52
Bhutan, 138–39
bicycle trip, 15
Big Ben, xvi, 37
Big Ben Problem, 37–38
big-box stores, 50
bike cards, 148
biking, 149
Birchbox, 85–86, 89, 97
Blair, Tony, 84
blogs, 19, 81, 85–86
BMWs, 28, 29, 30, 65
Bobb, Trevor, 23
Bock, Laszlo, 21, 69, 127
Bolivia, 121
bonuses, 127–29
books, 17
boredom, 48–49
Bosanek, Debbie, 151
brain, 92–93, 116, 151
Brand, Dan, 59
breaks, 42–44
Broadway, 9
"Bro Downs," 39

Buffett, Warren, xviii, 106, 110, 151
bullfighting, 22
bulls, 48
bundling, 96–97
Bureau of Labor Statistics, U.S., 136, 138
"Business Time," 21
busyness, 55–58
buyer's remorse, 16
buylesscrap.org, 131
Buy One, Get One Free, 145

cable, 66
California, 44
  bicycle trip through, 15
Calment, Jeanne, 36
Canada, xviii, 111–12, 143–44
cancer, 81
candy corn, 34
Card Case, 98–99
Carrey, Jim, 9
cars, 73, 137
  appreciation of, 32
  fast, 50
  luxury, xvi, 28–30, 65
car-sharing companies, 41–42
Carter, Travis, *10*, 15
cash, 99
cause marketing, 129–31
Cedar Rapids (film), 44–45
Census Bureau, U.S., 63
Central Park, 14
change, sensitivity to, 33
charities, 136
charity, 61, 75
  cause marketing and, 129–31
  happiness and, 106–7, 108–9
  taxes as, 152–53
  see also donations
charity vouchers, 105–6
Charlie and the Chocolate Factory (Dahl), 31–32
Charmin, 49
Chase, Robin, 41
cheerometers, 33, 46, 50
chemotherapy, 81
Chicago museum, 9
children, 68
  investing in others by, 114–15
China, 142, 155
Chinese State Council Information Office, 155
chocolate, xvii, 84–85, 88–89, 146
  abundance of, 27–28, 32
  declining enjoyment of, 34
  economic considerations and, 51–52
  pain of paying and, 92–93
  as treat, 31–32, 50
chores, 66
Christmas gifts, 118
  deadweight loss, 118
Chuck E. Cheese, 24
churches, 136
Cialdini, Robert, 40
cigarette taxes, 146
Cinderella (film), 40
cities, experience preferred to material goods in, 6
Classic Car Club, 4102
cleaning, 56
Clement, Jemaine, 21
Clinton, Bill, 84
CNN.com, xii–xiii
Coca-Cola, 39
coffee, xvi, 35–36
commercials, xvi, 42–43, 44
commuting, 63–64, 68, 137, 141, 148
concerts, xv, 5
connecting, 119
consulting, 78
consume now, pay later, xvii, 94–96
Consumer Electronics Association, 80
Consumer Financial Protection Bureau, 150
cooking, 56
Cornell University, 8–9, *10*
cortisol, 124–25
Cosmopolitan, 75
Costa Rica, 22
cotton, 124–25
county fair, 101

Crate & Barrel, 106, 119–20
credit cards, xvii, 79, 94–96
  average debt of, 95
  cash vs., 99
  declining use of, 97–98
CSI (TV show), 43
Cuisinart, 22
cultural institutions, 144–45
customers, xv, 22

Dalai Lama, 46
Danish Holiday Act, 145
Davis, Fred, 13
Dawes, Dave and Angela, 117–18
deadweight loss, 118
Dean, Will, xvi, 6–8
debit cards, 97–98
debts, 95–96
Declaration of Independence, 138
Deegan, Shannon, 69
delayed consumption, 86, 87–89
  healthy grocery shopping and, 99
  pleasure enhanced by, 91–92
  see also anticipation; pay now, consume later
delays, 89–92
Democrats, 140
Denmark, 142, 145, 147
depression, 55
desirability, 100
diary, 116
digital technology, 79–80
diminishing marginal utility, 66*n*
Diners Club card, 79
dinner out, 51
Disney, 40
divorce, 141
dodge ball, xii, 127–28
dogs, 62–63, 66
Dollar Collective, 123
donations, 127, 136
  mandatory, 116
  seeing impact of, 121–23
  see also charity
DonorsChoose.org, xix, 105–6, 119–20, 125
Double Down, 38–39, 58
driving, 149
  expenses of, 64–65
drool factor, 88–89
drooling, 87–89
Dumbo (film), 40
Dunn, Elizabeth:
  arctic road trip of, 14, 15
  Benjamin Effect studied by, 46–47
  and dog getting sprayed by skunk, 28
  free time desired by, 54
  Hawaiian trip of, 87
  ideal holiday of, 20
  lattes as treats for, 35–36
  used mattress purchased by, 72–73
  at yoga class, 56
Dusoulier, Clotilde, 19

East Africa, xii, 111–13
economic downturn, 97–98
economic growth, 142, 145*n*
eggnog, 34
ehoneymoonregistry.com, 22
elBulli, xii, 18–19
elderly:
  experience preferred to material goods by, 6
  life appreciated by, 36
email-free Tuesdays, 55–56
Eminem, 42
emotional connection, 119–20
employees, xv, 22
entertainment, 136
Eternal Sunshine of the Spotless Mind (film), 9, 12
Europe, happiness in, 141*n*
exercise:
  free time and, 56
  happiness and, 62
  mood and, 55
expectations, about spending 137–38
  see also positive expectations
experiential purchases:
  abstract benefits of, 22–23

experiential purchases (*cont.*)
  apples-and-oranges quality of, 16–17
  government incentives toward, 144–45
  memorability of, 13–15, 18, 20
  painful, xvi, 14–15
  and passage of time, 23–24
  as revealing "true, essential selves," 9, *10*, 20
  unique, 18–20, 20
experiential purchases, material purchases vs., xii, xv—xvi, 1–25, 135, 136, 143–45
  at Chuck E. Cheese, 24
  and connections with others, 7–8, 20, 22
  difficulty of distinguishing between, 17–18
  home-ownership and, xv, 1–4
  partnerships and, 8–9
  space tourism and, 1
  in wedding registry, 22

Facebook, 7–8, 23, 126
family, 63, 67
Fannie Mae, 143
fart jokes, 27, 32
fast-food logos, 60
feasibility, 100
Federal Election Commission, 152
Ferraris, 41
Fiamengo, John, 5, 20
Fiamengo, Marcia, 5, 20, 82–83, 133
Finland, 13
flat-screen TVs, 66
Flight of the Conchords, 21
Florida, 44, 45
food, 136
food banks, 116, 151
Ford Escort, 28, 30
forms, filling out, 59
Fortune, 70
Founding Fathers, 138
Four Seasons, 52
France, women in, 63, 69
Franklin, Benjamin, 76, 77
Frappuccinos, 90, 135, 136
Freddie Mac, 143
Frederick, Shane, 33
free time, 145
Friday, 81, 82
friends, 63, 67
fries, 50–51
Fuchs, Christopher "Kreece," 129
fund-raisers, 117
Funky Monkey, 22–23
future, pleasant thoughts about, 82

Gallup organization, 118
Gallup World Poll, 113
Gates, Bill, xviii
genes, 137
Germany, 2, 4
  commuting in, 63–64
  and money and time pressure, 56
Gibbard, Ben, 84
gift certificates, 135
  expiration dates on, 37–38
gifts, xviii, 84, 118–19, 123
  Christmas, 118
  happiness and, 108–9
Gilovich, Tom, *10*, 15
girlfriends, 118–19
Gmail, 69
Godiva chocolates, 84–85, 92–93
goldfish, 62
gold standard, 94
Google, xviii–xix
  awards given at, 21–22
  bonuses at, 127
  People Operations, 69
  time policy at, 69
Google Sky, 69
governments, 138–39, 154–55
gratitude, 30–31
Great Britain, 155
  debt in, 95
  taxation in, 149–150, 153
grocery shopping, 56
  with cash, 99
gross domestic product, 138
Gross National Happiness, 138
gyms, 101*n*

Habitat for Humanity, 61
Haines, Elizabeth, and husband, Terry, 47–48, 96–97
Halpern, David, 145–46, 154, 155
happiness:
  anticipation and, 91
  biking and, 149
  as boosted before travel, 81
  charitable donations and, 106–7
  on Christmas wish lists, 80
  exercise and, 62
  and fantasizing about the future, 82
  genes and, 137
  housing as unimportant to, 2–4, 6
  housing characteristics important to, 4*n*
  income and, xiv, 31, 95
  inequality linked to, 141–42, 151
  prosocial spending and, 108–13, 116, 119, 123
  spending on others and, 107
  voluntary simplicity and, 35–36
  see also money-happiness relationship
"Happiness Runs in a Circular Motion," 123
Harvard Business Review, xii
Harvard Business School, 85*n*
Harvard University:
  housing at, 2–4, 7*n*
  sabbatical program at, 70
Hawaii, 87, 88
Hawkins, Daniel, 123
health, improved by giving to others, 124
healthcare, 136
Helgesen, Xavier, 129
Helliwell, John, 155
Helms, Ed, 44
Hershey's Hug, 88, 89
Hershey's Kiss, 88, 89–90
Hinck, Kristine, 126
Hindustan Times, xii
Home Depot, xvii, 61
Hôtel de Glace, 13
housing, housing quality, 28, 50, 136, 137
  children and, 68
  considered important to Americans, xv, 4
  satisfaction with, 2, 4, 64
  social life in, 7*n*
  as unimportant to happiness, 1, 2–4, 6, 7*n*, 21, 68
housing meltdown, 1, 4, 143
humor, 87
hypocrisy, xi

iamToddyTickles, 38
Ice Hotel, 13
ice hotels, 13, 14
inaction, regret over, 16
income:
  happiness related to, xiv, 31, 95
  rising, 58
Indianapolis, 133
inequality, 139–41
  unhappiness linked to, 141–42, 151
Influence (Cialdini), 40
insula, 93
insurance, 136
Intel, xvii
  email-free Tuesdays at, 55–56
  sabbaticals at, 70
intelligence, 9
Internal Revenue Service, 149
intuition, failures of, xix
investing in others, xviii, 105–33, 135, 136, 151–53
  health improved by, 124
  in poor countries, 110–13
iPads, 80
iPhones, 16
Irazabal, Ami, 126
Ireland, 45
irrigation pumps, 122
irritation, 55
isolation, xiii, xv
Italy, 45, 142, 151
iTunes, 102

Jacobs, Joanne, 59
Japan, 151
Jetsons, The, 53, 54
Jigme Singye Wangchuck, King of Bhutan, 138–39
Johnson, Cami, 24

kaleidoscope, 32–33
karmacurrency.com.au, 127
Kayak.com, 92
Kensington Palace, 37
KFC, 38–39
Kickstart, 122
kisses, 91
Klein, Alan, 39–40
Kmart, 133
Knack, 43
Krueger, Alan, 142
Kurtz, Jaime, 36

labor illusion, 92
landmarks, 37
Las Vegas, Nev., 45
lattes, xvi, 50
Latvia, 148
laughter, 87
leaking roofs, 4*n*
Lee, Derek, 40–41
"Legends of the McRib" event, 40
Leverett House Bunny, 3
libertarians, 154
"life stories," 9
lines, waiting in, 54, 75
little pleasures, 31, 50
Live Near Your Work, 148
Loewenstein, George, 33
London, xvi, 37, 148
long-term relationship, 118–19
"Lose Yourself" (song), 43
Lost (TV show), 43
lottery, xiii, xv, 51, 100, 117–18

McDonald's, 39–40, 50–51
McRib sandwich, 39–40, 42
McSalad Shaker, 59–60
magazine ads, 75–76
Make a Connection, 115, 117–21
Make an Impact, 115, 121–23
Make It a Choice, 115, 116–17
makeup, xviii, 85-86
malaria, xviii, 111
malaria nets, 122
Manjoo, Farhad, 98
marginal utility, 66*n*
marriage, debt detrimental to, 95–96
Marriott, 13, 14
Martini, Kristen, 35
Maseratis, 41
massages, xv, 43–44, 52, 100–101
MasterCard, 79
material purchases:
  buyer's remorse about, 16–17
  experiential purchases vs., *see* experiential purchases, material purchases vs.
  and passage of time, 23–24
  selves not revealed by, 9, *10*
maternity leave, 76
mattresses, used, 72–73
maxing out, 66*n*
MBAs, 94–95
meals, xv—xvi, 5, 67
meaninglessness, 13
memorability, 13–15, 18, 20
memory, 9, 12
men, experience preferred to material goods by, 6
mercury, 33, 34, 46
Messing, Barbara, 83
Mexico, 97
Meyvis, Tom, 43–44
Michigan, University of, 28–30, 130
Milan, Italy, 148
Minard, Paulette, 61
Mini Cooper, 40–41
Missouri, 146
Mogolov, David, 64, 65
Mogolov, Lisa, 64, 65
mojitos, xviii
Monday, 82
money:
  mind-set promoted by, 74–75

thoughts of, as counterproductive to happiness, xiv—xv, 31, 32
time as, 76–78
time value of, 102
money constraints, 71
money-happiness relationship, xi, xii
counterproductive strategies in, xiii
mistakes about, xiv
and purchase of time, 55
in various countries, 142–43
mood:
as affected by commuting, 64, 68
as affected by friends and family, 67
as affected by work, 68–69
Morrison, Dennis, 53
Morrison, Kathleen, 53, 59
moving, 81
Mulago Foundation, 121
Murphy, David, 129–30
museums, 144
music, 77
Myers, David, 139
Myers, Lisa, 70
"My Sharona" (song), 43

National Australia Bank, 127
National Center for Family Literacy, 129
national parks, 144
neighbors, 4*n*, 59
Nelson, Leif, 43–44
Netherlands, 81, 142
taxation in, 153
transportation in, 148–49
neuroeconomists, 92–93
New Jersey, 65
Newsweek, 36
New York, 146
New York, 67
New York, N.Y., 40, 44, 65, 148
New Yorker, 75
New York Times, 151
New Zealand, 21
next-day delivery, 79
Nicaragua, 20
Nooyi, Indra, 126
North Carolina, University of, 122
Norton, Michael, 43
albums preordered by, 102
bullfighting tickets bought by, 22
in Canadian customs incident, 131–32
charity voucher received by, 105–6, 119
at elBulli restaurant, 8
extensive traveling by, 71–72
favorite treats of, 34
free time desired by, 54
ideal holiday of, 20
paid consulting gigs turned down by, 78
"Sometimes" (song), 43
nostalgia, 13, 18
Notre Dame University, 129
novelty, 29, 46–50
now, power of, 90
Now and Laters, 102
nucleus accumbens, 82, 93

Obama, Barack, 142, 151, 152
Obama, Michelle, 151
obesity, 149
Office, The (TV show), 42–43
Office of Planning, 148
Ohio, 4
Old North Church, 45–46
olfactory fatigue, 28
Onion, 54, 94, 156
online dating, 84
open-mindedness, 9
optimizing, 66*n*
Oregon, University of, 116
Orlando, Fla., 45
outgoingness, 9
overconsumption, 146

Pagano, Barbara, 70–71
Pagano, Elizabeth, 70–71
pain of paying, 92–93
Paris, 17, 45, 50–51
parks, 144

partners, as preferred by people who like experiential purchases, 8–9
Patagonia, xvii
pay now, consume later, xvii, 79–103, 136, 149–150
child-care and, 96–97
debit cards and, 97–99
sunk cost problem and, 101–2
pay-per-performance, 129
Pay with Square, 98–99
peace, 80
"peak car," 63
Pennsylvania, University of, 75
pens, xv, 16–17
pensions, 136
People Operations, 69
peppermint stick ice cream, 34
PepsiCo, xviii–xix, 126
Pepsi Refresh Project, 126
personal spending, 109–10
prosocial spending ratio with, 109–10, 133
Peter Pan (film), 40
pets, 62
pharmaceutical sales, 128
Philadelphia, Pa., 50–51
Pilot G2 Super Fine pen, 16–17
piñata, 128
pleasure, 82
political debates, 87–88
popcorn, 49–50
port-a-potties, 49
positive expectations, 87–89, 93
Postal Service, 84
Potty Palooza, 49
power of now, 90
praying, 55
prepaying, 96–97
presidents, approval ratings of, 84
prom, 9
prosocial spending, 108–9, 120–21
cause marketing, 129–31
as choice, 116–17, 123
in dodgeball league, 127–29
happiness and, 108–13, 116, 119, 123
by National Australia Bank, 127
by Pepsi, 126
personal spending ratio with, 109–10, 133
Protestant work ethic, 51
prune juice, 89
psychological health, 82
puppies, 36

Quebec, 13

Radcliffe Quad, 3
reading, 55
Red Hots, 34
refrigerators, 6, 66
regret, over inaction, 16
relationships, long-term, 118–19
renting, 4, 6
Republicans, 40
requests, 117
Restaurant Rejuvenation Act, 146–47
reward, 82
Romania, 13
Romantic Love Symptom Checklist, 48
romantic partners, 46–49, 50
Roombas, 53, 58–59
rural areas, experience preferred to material goods in, 6

sabbatical programs, 70–71
SailTime, 42
salary, 76–77
saliva, xii, xviii
Salivette, 124
same-day delivery, 79
San Francisco, Calif., 59, 75
sangria, 83, 84, 88
Sarah Silverman Program, The (TV show), 27
Sarstedt company, 124
Saskatchewan, Canada, 61
Saturday Night Live, 27
savings, 96
goals, 137–38
scarcity, 58
scarcity marketing, 38–41
Scooba, 53
Seinfeld, 92

self-denial, xvi, 99
self-discipline, 91
selves:
memory and, 9
as revealed by experiential purchases, 9, *10*, 20
Seneca, 15
se réjouir, 80–81, 83, 88
sex, 55
sexual problems, 59
shame, 125
shampoo, 59
sharing, 114–15
Shulman, Doug, 149
Silverman, Sarah, 27
Silverman's Mantra, 27, 32, 40, 50, 145
Singapore, 148, 151
Slate, 67
Slow Movement, 57
smartphones, 16
Smits, Emily, 116
soap, 146
social connections, experiences and, 7–8, 20
socializing, 63, 67, 67–68, 74, 75
soda, 89, 147
Somerville, Mass., 139, 144
"Sometimes" (song), 43
South Africa, 4*n*, 147
Southern California, University of, 88
South Korea, 147
and money and time pressure, 56
space tourism, 1–2, 5, 16, 19–20, 45, 82–83, 89, 133
Spain, 22
spa treatments, 51, 52, 83, 100
spouses, 46–49, 50
Spread the Net, 121–22
Starbucks, 90, 119, 120, 135
Starr, Kevin, 121, 122
Stockholm City Bikes, 148
stone disks, 93–94
strawberries, 18, 45
Stroessner, Steve, 24
subprime mortgages, 143
suburbs, experience preferred to material goods in, 6
suicide, 82
Summerville, Amy, 101–2
Sundays, 81–82
sunk costs, 101–2
Super Bowl, 126
Sweden, 13, 151
swimming pools, 73–74
Sydney, Australia, 46

Tamborello, Jimmy, 84
Target, 98
taxes, 76, 149–50, 151–53
as charity, 152–53
equality and, 151–52
taxis, 96
Teacher Barbie, 80–81
teamwork, 7–8
telephones, 66
television, xvi, 73
declining enjoyment of, 32
time spent doing, 63, 65–67
10 Downing Street, 139
tension, 55
Tequila Tuesday, 7*n*
thank-you notes, 120
thermometers, 33, 34, 50
time:
buying, xvi–xvii, 53–78, 135, 136, 147–49
fading enjoyment and, 32–33, 34
mind-set promoted by, 74–76
as money, 76–78, 101
wrinkle in, 81
time, free, 53–54
past vs. present, 57
time affluence, xvii, 55–56
time-saving products and reductions in, 60
as undermined by commuting, 64
volunteer work and increases in, 60–61, 125
time constraints, 71
time diaries, 57
time pressure, increased by wealth,

56–58
time-saving products, time affluence reduced by, 60
toasters, 22
toddlers, 114–15
toilet paper, 49, 50
Tokyo, 45
tolls, 148
Tonight Show with Jay Leno, The, xii
toothpaste, 146
Toronto, University of, 58
"Total Touch" toaster, 22
Tough Mudder, xvi, 6–8, 22–23, 86, 117
trains, 65
transportation, 136, 137
travel, xv, 5, 9, 44–46
  extensive, 71–72
  happiness boosted before, 81
  in space, 1–2, 5, 16, 19–20, 45, 82–83, 89, 133
Traveler's Joy, 22
Travellerspoint, 46
treats, xvi, 27–52, 136, 145–47
  altering pattern of, 34–36
  chocolate as, 31–32
  commercials and, xvi, 42–43, 44
  driving as, 30
  lattes as, 35–36
  novelty and, 29, 46–50
  scarcity marketing and, 38–41
  travel as, 44–46
TripAdvisor.com, 83, 88, 89
TripWatch emails, 83
Turkey, 56
Twain, Mark, 16, 120
Twitter, 38, 81, 85

Uganda, xviii, 111–13
U-index, 54–55, 63, 66
uncertainty, 85–86
UNICEF (United Nations Children's Fund), 121
United Nations Conference on Happiness, 139, 155
United Nations General Assembly, 139
United States:
  home-owning considered important in, xv, 4
  income in, xiv
  inequality in, 139–42
  money-happiness relationship in, 142
  time affluence research in, 56
  transportation in, 148
  women in, 63, 69
unpleasant moods, 54–55
utility, 66*n*

vacuuming, vacuums, 53, 58–59, 71
Valentine's Day, 47, 123
Venice, Italy, 22
Virgin Galactic, 1, 5, 16, 20, 82–83, 133
Virginia, University of, 84–85
Visa, 94
Vivenes, David, 39
Volkswagen Beetle, 41
voluntary simplicity, 35
volunteering, 74
volunteer work, 56
  as less likely by hourly workers, 78
  time affluence increased by, 60–61, 125

wages, 77–78
Waldfogel, Joel, 118
walking, 149
watches, 14
wealth:
  increased by investing in others, 124
  little pleasures and, 31
  time pressure increased by, 56–58
wealth distribution, xi
wedding registry, 22
weddings, 97, 117–18
weight gain, 4
White House Council of Economic

Advisers, 142
Williams, R. Neil, 94
Winfrey, Oprah, 30–31
Winslet, Kate, 9
women:
experience preferred to material goods by, 5–6
pleasure received by, 63
workforce entered by, 57
and work's effect on mood, 68–69
work, 68–71
World Happiness Report, 155
Wounded Warrior Project, 117
wrinkle in time, 81

Yale University, 32–33
Yap, 93–94
Yellowstone National Park, 70
Yingling, Ashlee, 39
yoga, 56
young people:
abundance sought by, 36
experience preferred to material goods by, 6
YourSabbatical.com, 70
YouTube, 85

Zauberman, Gal, 71
Zipcars, 41

About the Authors

ELIZABETH DUNN is an associate professor of psychology at the University of British Columbia in Vancouver, Canada. At age twenty-six, she was featured as one of the "rising stars" across all of academia by the *Chronicle of Higher Education.* Her work has been featured in top academic journals, including two recent papers in *Science,* and in hundreds of media outlets worldwide.

MICHAEL NORTON is an associate professor of marketing at Harvard Business School. His research has twice been featured in the *New York Times Magazine* Year in Ideas issue. In 2012, he was selected for *Wired* magazine's Smart List as one of "50 People Who Will Change the World."